The Encyclopedia of Canvas Embroidery Stitch Patterns

THE ENCYCLOPEDIA OF
Canvas Embroidery Stitch Patterns

KATHARINE IREYS

Thomas Y. Crowell Company　　NEW YORK · ESTABLISHED 1834

Acknowledgment is made to the following:

Charles Scribner's Sons for Binding Stitch from Hope Hanley's *New Methods in Needlepoint,* 1968.

The Embroiderers' Guild for Interlaced Stitch from "New Stitches for Canvas Embroidery" by John Gleave in *Embroidery,* Summer 1971.

B. T. Batsford Ltd. for Rhodes Stitch from Mary Rhodes's *Ideas for Canvas Work,* 1970.

Designed by Jill Schwartz

MANUFACTURED IN THE UNITED STATES OF AMERICA

L.C. Card 72-78267 ISBN 0-690-26336-8
1 2 3 4 5 6 7 8 9 10

PREFACE

Most books on embroidery contain some stitch patterns, a chapter on color and design, some directions for make-up, some history, etc., but nothing is complete. This book attempts to cover one phase of embroidery and do it thoroughly. It contains almost all known stitch patterns for canvas embroidery. There are diagrams and directions for 170 stitch patterns, many variations, some borrowed from surface stitchery. I have tried to cover this one phase completely, gathering together in one book all the stitch patterns scattered through the many books that treat all phases of embroidery.

The stitch patterns are divided rather loosely into four classes, the simplest first, and the most complex at the last part of each section.

Straight	pages	1–24
Crossed	pages	25–87
Diagonal	pages	88–117
Miscellaneous	pages	118–155

Although these stitch patterns are planned mostly for single mesh (mono) canvas, they can be equally effective on double mesh (Penelope) canvas. Several of them can be done only on the double mesh canvas.

NAMES

I have tried to include all the names for each stitch pattern and to cross-index them. However, there is such confusion in names that it is almost impossible to include them all. For instance, there is one stitch pattern called Diagonal Florentine, or Florence. This is really Parisian on the diagonal, so some people call it Diagonal Parisian. Then there are some books that call it Cashmere. But there is another stitch pattern called Cashmere. . . . I've done the best I could.

TERMS

"Horizontal" and "vertical" need no explanation.

"Diagonal" is used to indicate only a 45° angle. Any other angle is called "slanting."

"Thread" is used to indicate the canvas threads only.

"Strand" or "yarn" is used to indicate the material being sewed into, or laid on the canvas.

"Journey" means 1 trip across a row.

"Compensation" means the use of the part of a unit of a stitch pattern at the edge where the whole unit would extend past the area being covered.

The word "stitch" has three distinct meanings:

1. It is a length of yarn on the surface, from where it comes out from the back to where it goes in again.
2. It is also the insertion of the needle, bringing it to the surface again and pulling the working strand through.
3. It also means the different arrangements of stitches (definition 1) into patterns. We speak of a cross stitch and a buttonhole stitch, etc. I have tried to eliminate the third meaning by substituting "stitch pattern," but with very little success.

"Plucking" refers to half of a stitch (definition 2), in which the worker inserts the needle, and pulls the working strand through to the back. Then the needle is brought up to the surface in a separate motion. Many beginners use this method, but, except for a few instances, it is not advised.

DIAGRAMS

The stitch patterns are shown in two forms of diagrams. The ones on the right with the circles, arrows, dotted lines, and needle in position are very specific. They show exactly where to begin, where every stitch goes, and the direction of the needle on the back. Some stitches are numbered. The symbol for the stitch O⟶ shows where the needle comes out from the back and where it goes in again. The shaft of the arrow is the stitch. With a little practice you will be able to interpret these diagrams easily.

The diagrams on the left more nearly resemble the finished work. They look as if they had been worked with yarn too fine for the canvas so the canvas threads are showing. In reality these threads would be covered by the stitches, which is necessary in all canvas work. But the diagrams are clearer if they are drawn with the canvas threads exposed. Only worked samples will give you a true picture.

HOW TO USE THE STITCH PATTERNS IN DESIGNING

First, beautiful effects can be obtained by simple striping; no design needed. There are two distinct ways to design for canvas stitchery:

1. Geometric. In geometric designs the different patterns are fitted together with little or no compensation. This usually requires careful planning on graph paper. Consider the lines on the paper the canvas threads, and the white squares the holes. Draw the stitches from the center of one white square to the center of another. Indicate your colors on the paper. Little or no marking is necessary on the canvas.

2. For all other designing—abstract, literal (pictures of things), etc.—make a drawing on plain white paper. Go over the lines with a broad felt tip marker. Place the canvas over the drawing, and the lines will show through. Trace with thinned oil paint or acrylics, a ball point pen, laundry marking pen, or *waterproof* India ink, using a fine brush or a steel pen in a holder. Make the lines as fine as possible. Do *not* use felt tip markers or pens. Even those so-called waterproof ones can stain the yarn when the piece is blocked.

Little or no color is needed on the canvas; it is not necessary to paint it. Color your drawing after selecting the yarn you need. The fine lines on the canvas will be enough to guide you.

Keep in mind the texture of the different stitch patterns. Some are flat and smooth, some are high, nubby, ridged, fuzzy. It seems logical to use a large fairly loose stitch, such as Bricking, for the background, using some of the smaller unit stitches for the design so as to minimize distortion, and include as much detail as possible. But this produces a piece with large, rather fluffy, stitches in the background, and an indented design. The reverse is really what you want, a high-textured design, and a smooth flat background. Adapt your design so as to use the more decorative stitches, and save the smaller flat stitches for background.

Keep away from realism as much as possible. The simplest design will take on great beauty when worked in a variety of stitch patterns. For example, a flower form with a center of French Knots, or Tufting, or a Spider Web.

Curves. There are only four stitch patterns that will actually curve: simple Couching, Chain, Split, and Van Dyke. Rows of the Chain pattern can be used to cover an area where curves are desired.

Outlining. Sometimes outlining adds much to a design. The best stitches for this are the same four as for curves. Work other patterns right up to each other, and put your outline along the line where they meet.

Radiating lines. Radiating lines are hard to achieve with canvas stitch patterns without a lot of distortion. You can work surface stitchery on top of your background, such as Detatched Chain (Lazy Daisy). You can use outline or Split stitch for fine lines.

Canvas stitchery can be combined with surface stitchery (Crewel) quite effectively. The stitch patterns can be varied greatly. We are seeing more and more free designing of canvas pieces that are works of art in their own right. Talented artists are exploring this form of stitchery with splendid results. All the rules can be broken. Even weave material can be substituted for the canvas, and parts left exposed.

There's really no limit to the possibilities. So let yourself go, and have fun.

Three final suggestions.

Be sure to bind your single mesh canvas first. It frays terribly. Although self-sticking tape is widely used as a binding, it is not nearly as satisfactory as cloth binding put on with a sewing machine. This holds up well through all the handling, and stays in place through washing and blocking. Allow an inch to an inch and a half of plain unworked canvas along all sides. This gives you a place for the tacks used in blocking. The bound edge can be cut away, if necessary, when the piece is mounted.

The easiest way to fill an irregular shape is to work a row across the widest area. Then work to the bottom, compensating along the sides as you go. Now turn your work halfway around (top to bottom). Fitting a row up to your first row, work to the bottom again. This is much easier than trying to start with complicated compensating along an irregular edge.

For left-handed people, there are special directions for many of the stitches. They are indicated by an asterisk and appear after the regular directions. An additional hint to these people: If you find reversing the "left" and "right" of right-handed directions too confusing, you may find it easier to give your work a one-fourth turn counterclockwise, and work the right-handed directions in vertical rows. In most cases you will find this as convenient as the "top-to-bottom" turn, or the left-right reversal.

I hope this book will prove useful and will widen your knowledge and enjoyment of canvas embroidery.

K. S. I.

Florentine, scallop design

Hungarian Ground

Hungarian (top) and Double Hungarian

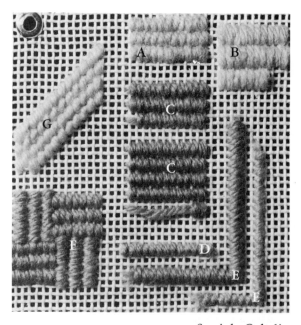

Straight Gobelin

A. Plain (over 2 threads) B. Plain (over 3 threads) C. Padded Gobelin D. Padded Gobelin (over 1 thread) E. Mitered corners (over 1 and 2 threads) F. Plain (over 2 threads), Parquetry Design G. Diagonal

A SELECTION OF CROSS STITCH PATTERNS

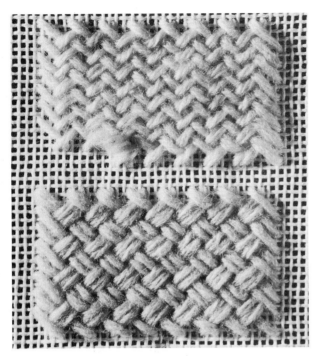

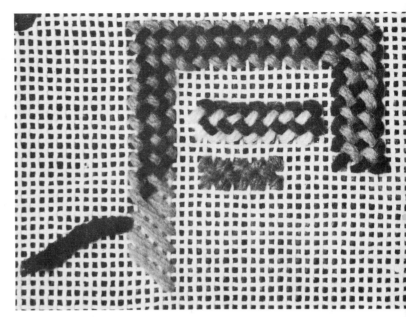

Woven Band

Herringbone (top) and Herringbone-Gone-Wrong

Double Herringbone (top) and Herringbone Couching

Large Oblong Cross (small size on Penelope canvas)

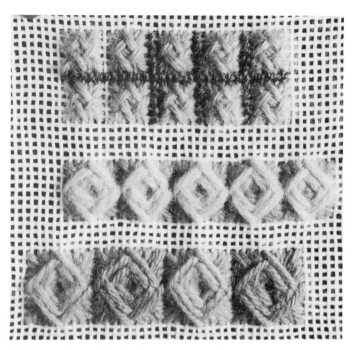

Waffle or Norwich (units over 5, 7, and 9 threads)

Double Straight Cross

Multistep Herringbone

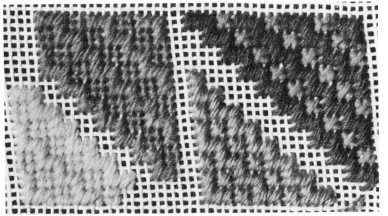

Diagonal Hungarian Ground

Oriental Variation

Hobnail (top) and Dotted Swiss

Cushion

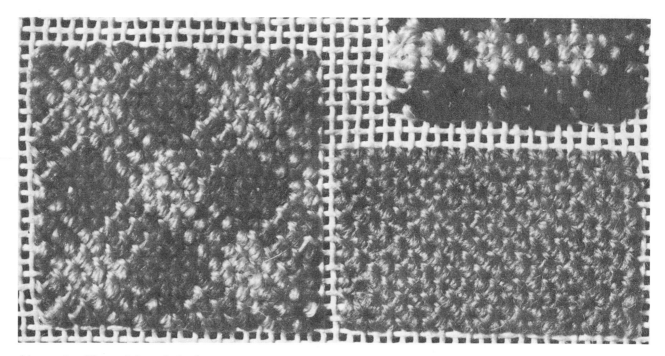

Alternating Tent, plain and check

Diagonal Tent, plaid design

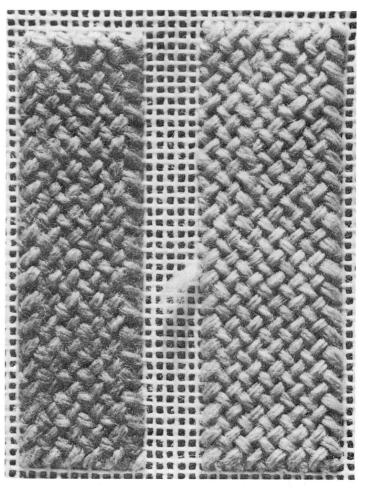

Diagonal Weaving

A SELECTION OF MISCELLANEOUS STITCH PATTERNS

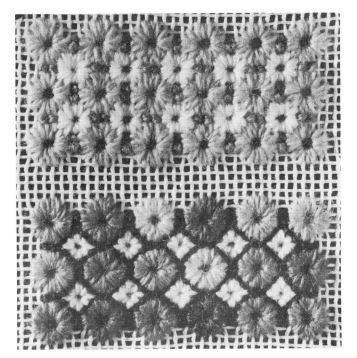

Algerian Eye Variations

Shadow Box (top) and Stacked Cubes

Spider Webs

Tip of Leaf

Geometric design using Padded Gobelin, Cross Stitch with Bar, Reverse Tent, Diagonal Cross, Double Straight Cross, Straight Cross, and Cross-Stitch-Gone-Wrong

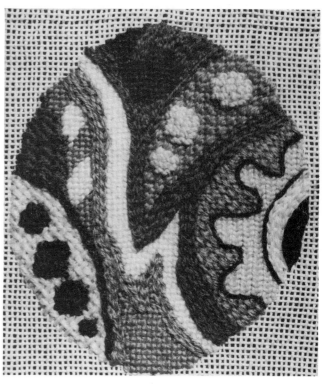

Abstract design using Tent, Chain, Split, Diagonal Weaving, Cross-Stitch-Gone-Wrong, Reverse Tent, French Knots, Hungarian, Diagonal Parisian, and Mosaic

Striped design using Cushion 2, Padded Gobelin, Rice, Waffle, Reverse Tent, and Diagonal Weaving

Border design using Florentine, Rice, and Padded Gobelin

Striped design using Cushion 2, Padded Gobelin, Reverse Tent, Rice, and Diagonal Weaving

Geometric design using Diamond Eye Variation, Tip of Leaf, Diamond Ray, Mosaic, Tent, and Diagonal Cross

Geometric design using Leaf, Chain, Double Straight Cross, and Tent

All photographs by Harry S. Coughanour

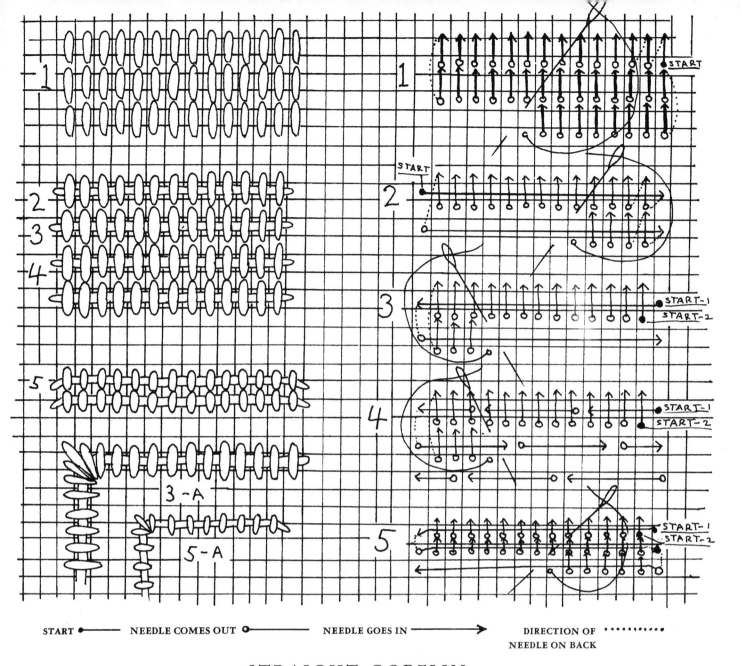

START ●————— NEEDLE COMES OUT ○————— NEEDLE GOES IN ————→ DIRECTION OF ·············
                                                            NEEDLE ON BACK

STRAIGHT GOBELIN

Diagrams 1 show the simplest form of Straight Gobelin. Each stitch covers 2 threads and every hole is used. Rows alternate in direction. Use heavy yarn and leave stitches fairly loose.

The right diagram 2 shows Padded Gobelin made with one working strand.

The right diagram 3 shows Padded Gobelin made with two working strands. The thickness of the strands can be varied to suit the canvas.

The right diagram 4 (tramé) can be used when a large area is to be covered. Laid strands are completed before covering stitches are done. Vary positions of laid strands so "breaks" will not be close to each other. They can be *much* longer than those in the diagram.

The left diagram 2, 3, 4 shows how these stitch patterns would look.

Diagrams 5 show small size, the covering stitches passing over laid strand and only 1 canvas thread.

Diagrams 3-A and 5-A show how to miter corners.

Forms 2, 3, and 5 make good edging. Although it is not indicated in the diagrams, these stitches completely cover the canvas.

1

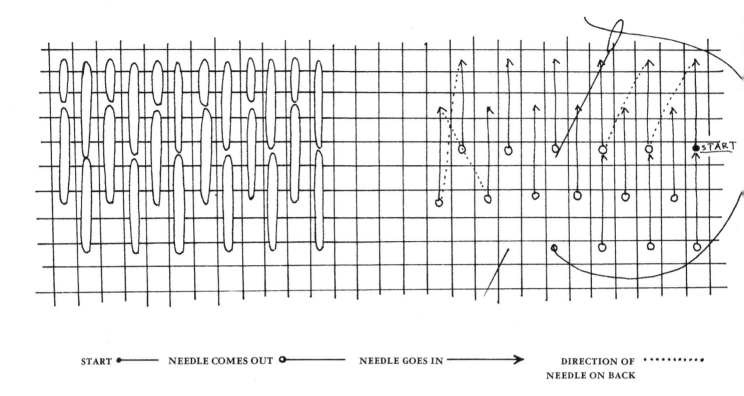

START ●━━━━━ NEEDLE COMES OUT ○━━━━━ NEEDLE GOES IN ━━━━━▶ DIRECTION OF ··········
                                                           NEEDLE ON BACK

BRICKING

Work vertical stitches in horizontal rows, covering 4 threads, using every other hole. The second row stitches encroach over 2 threads of the first row, using spaces between stitches of first row. The third row is directly under first row, using same hole for top of stitch. The diagram at the left shows compensating stitches at the top for a straight edge. Viewed from the side, this forms a brick pattern.

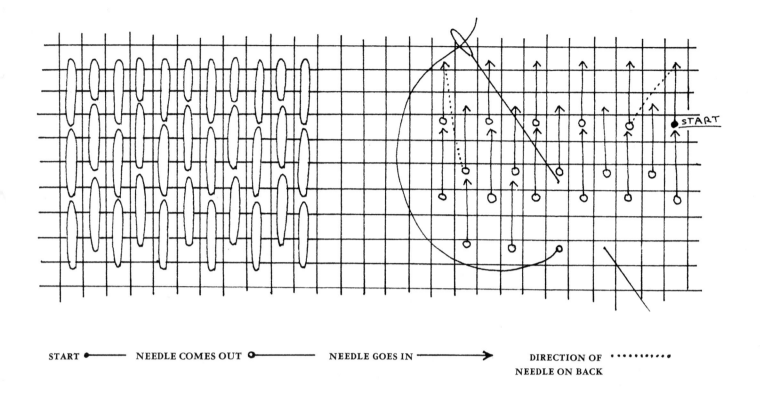

START ●—— NEEDLE COMES OUT O—— NEEDLE GOES IN ————▶ DIRECTION OF ••••••••••• NEEDLE ON BACK

UPRIGHT GOBELIN

Work vertical stitches in horizontal rows, covering 3 threads, using every other hole. The second row stitches encroach over 1 thread of the first row, using spaces between stitches of first row. The third row stitches encroach over 2 threads of second row. The fourth row stitches encroach over 1 thread, etc. The diagram at the left shows compensating stitches at the top for a straight edge.

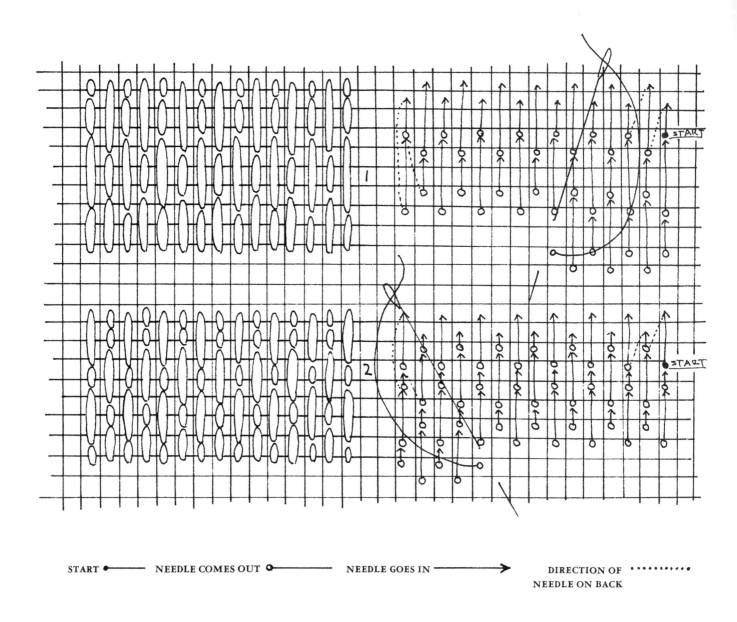

START •————— NEEDLE COMES OUT ○————— NEEDLE GOES IN ——————→ DIRECTION OF •••••••••
NEEDLE ON BACK

PARISIAN

Diagrams 1 show stitches made over 2, 4, 2, 4, 2, etc., threads. The long stitches of the second row fit under the short stitches of the first row and vice versa.

Diagrams 2 show stitches made over 1, 3, 1, 3, 1, etc., threads. The diagrams at left show compensating stitches at top and bottom.

Note: When using the 1, 3, 1, 3 count be sure to use heavy yarn and leave the stitches fairly loose.

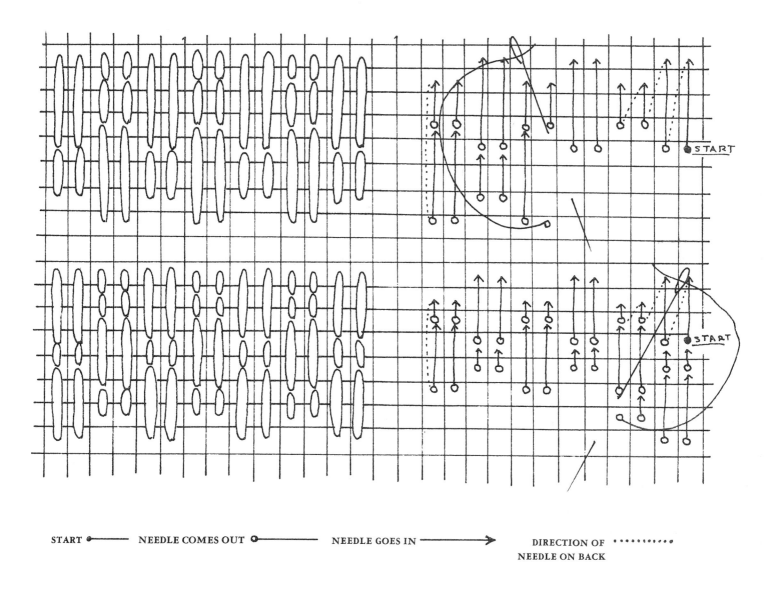

DOUBLE PARISIAN

Instead of covering 2, 4, 2, 4, etc., horizontal threads as in the Parisian stitch in preceding page, this stitch covers 2, 2, 4, 4, 2, 2, etc., threads. The same principle is applied to the 1, 3, 1, 3, etc., series. The sequence is 1, 1, 3, 3, 1, 1, etc. This principle can be extended to three or more stitches in a group.

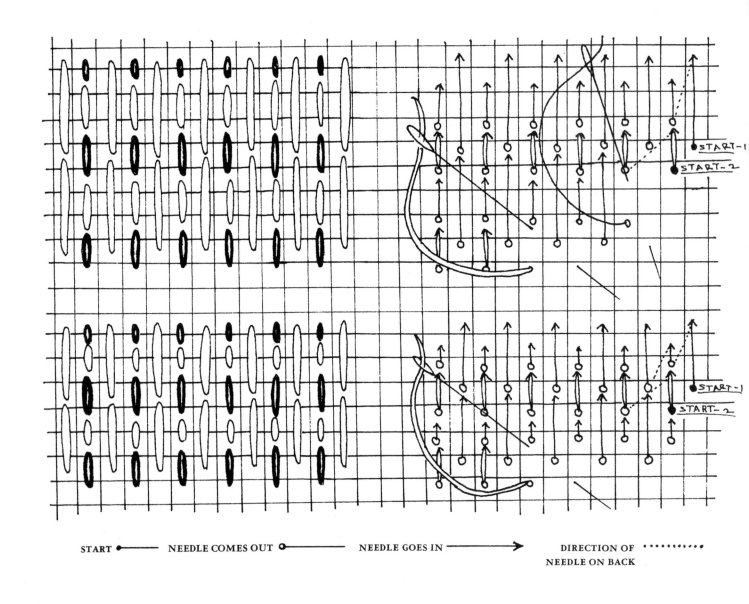

START ●——— NEEDLE COMES OUT ○——— NEEDLE GOES IN ———→ DIRECTION OF ••••••••••
NEEDLE ON BACK

PARISIAN & GOBELIN

Work first row in regular Parisian (p. 4), covering either the 2, 4, 2 threads or the 1, 3, 1, 3. Work the second row so that the long stitches come under those of the first row. This leaves spaces of 2 horizontal threads between rows. Cover these with Straight Gobelin (p. 1) stitches in a contrasting color.

This stitch pattern can be worked in one color. Make Parisian rows from right to left, and Gobelin rows from left to right. The diagrams at left show compensating stitches at the top for straight edges.

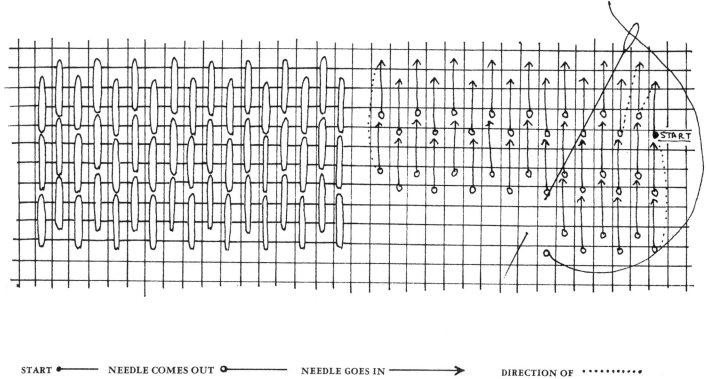

START ●━━━━━ NEEDLE COMES OUT ○━━━━━ NEEDLE GOES IN ━━━━▶ DIRECTION OF ••••••••••
NEEDLE ON BACK

LONG STRAIGHT
Florentine Variation

This Florentine variation is a form of Gobelin stitch. Vertical stitches cover 2, 3, or 4 horizontal threads. The rows are horizontal but the stitches step up and down 1 thread. The second row fits up under the first. All stitches are the same length. This stitch pattern makes a good background. It can be worked in stripes of several colors. It is also good for shading.

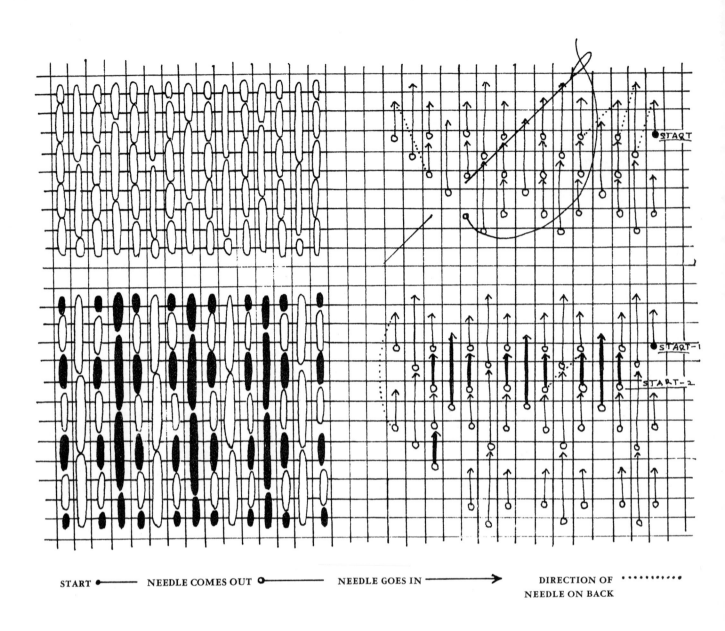

START •——— NEEDLE COMES OUT ○——— NEEDLE GOES IN ——————▶ DIRECTION OF ••••••••••
NEEDLE ON BACK

HUNGARIAN

The 3 stitches in each unit cover 2, 4, 2 threads. Then 2 threads (1 hole) are skipped before starting next unit. The long stitches in second row fit halfway up into spaces left between units of first row. All long stitches and all short stitches are directly under each other.

The diagrams at the top show stitch pattern worked in one color, the rows alternating right to left and left to right.

The diagrams at the bottom show rows worked in contrasting colors. Rows 1 and 2 are worked from right to left, and rows 3 and 4 are worked from left to right. Work one color at a time.

The diagrams at left show compensation for straight edges.

For geometric designing, these units fit against a diagonal line without compensation.

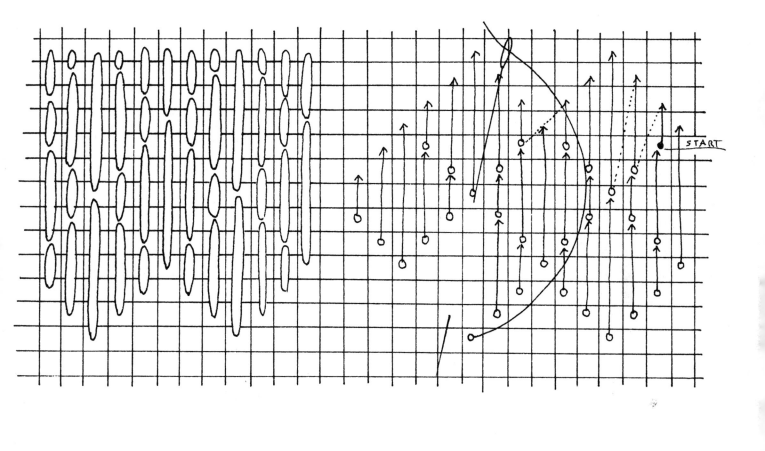

START ●——— NEEDLE COMES OUT ⊶————— NEEDLE GOES IN ————▶ DIRECTION OF ···········
NEEDLE ON BACK

HUNGARIAN VARIATION 1

The units are made up of vertical stitches covering 2, 4, 6, 4, 2—2, 4, 6, 4, 2 horizontal threads, adding 1 at top and bottom with each stitch. The units of the second row fit up under those of the first row. There are many possibilities for design by varying the colors of stitches or units.

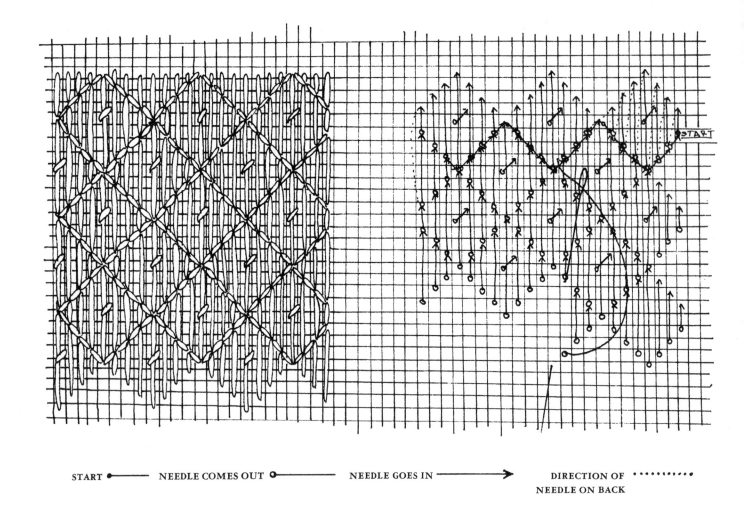

START •————— NEEDLE COMES OUT ○————— NEEDLE GOES IN ——————→ DIRECTION OF •••••••••
NEEDLE ON BACK

2, 4, 6, 8, & TIE
Hungarian Variation 2

This is really another variation of Hungarian. Make vertical stitches over 2, 4, 6, 8, 6, 4, 2 horizontal threads, adding 1 at top and 1 at bottom each time. Leave 2 threads (1 hole) between units. Longest stitch of second row uses this hole. Using finer yarn, make tie stitch 4 threads down on longest stitch and 1 intersection up, right. Back stitches (p. 137) over 1 intersection each are placed between units, using finer yarn.

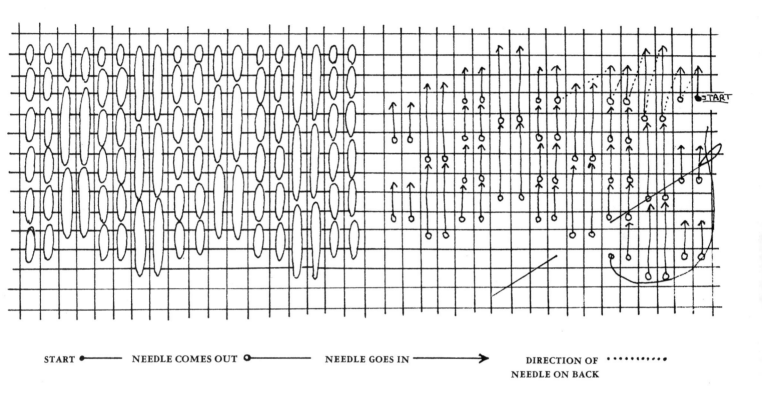

START ●——— NEEDLE COMES OUT o——— NEEDLE GOES IN ———→ DIRECTION OF •••••••••
NEEDLE ON BACK

DOUBLE HUNGARIAN

The units are composed of stitches covering 2, 2, 4, 4, 2, 2 threads. Skip 3 threads (2 holes), then 2, 2, 4, 4, 2, 2 again. The long stitches of second row fit halfway up into the space left between units of first row. The diagram at left shows compensation for straight edges at the top and sides.

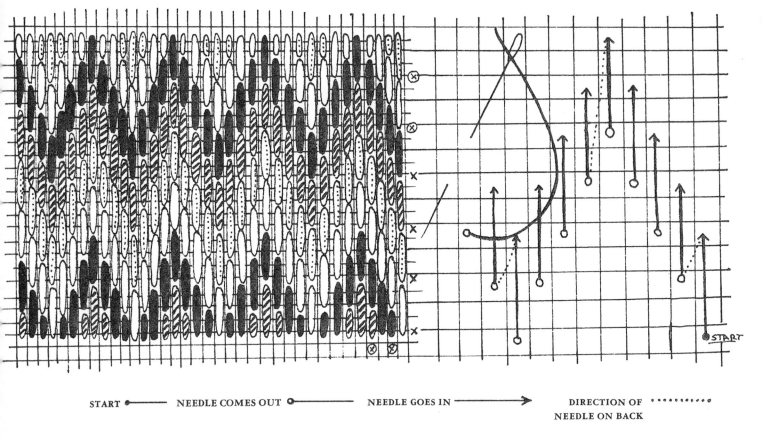

START ●━━ NEEDLE COMES OUT ○━━ NEEDLE GOES IN ━━━▶ DIRECTION OF ••••••••• NEEDLE ON BACK

FLORENTINE (BARGELLO)
Flame Stitch

The simplest form of Florentine, or Bargello, sometimes also called Flame stitch, is a series of stitches, each one covering four threads. These overlap two threads either up or down to form peaks and valleys. Many patterns can be formed using this size stitch, and varying the number of threads in the overlap to form scallops, different size peaks, etc. Beautiful effects can be obtained by using several shades of one color in stripes, with, perhaps, a contrasting color between sets. The left diagram shows gradation of four shades of one color, going from dark to light, and then starting with dark again. Start first row of each shade at the right X . At the end of the row at the left side, do not finish off the strand, but leave yarn hanging loose. Do this with each shade. When you are ready to start the next set of rows, they will be worked from left to right. The loose strands can be carried down the side and used to start these rows. Do the same when you arrive at the right side again.

The left diagram shows compensation at the top and bottom for straight edges. It is a good idea to work these rows after the main body of the work is done. Start at ⊗

There are more elaborate forms of Florentine, using stitches of different lengths. The possibilities for patterns are endless. The only thing they all have in common is that they all use vertical stitches.

Some sources of additional patterns:

Canvas Embroidery, by Hebe Cox. London: Mills and Boon Limited. (Address: 50 Grafton Way, Fitzroy Square, London W 1, England)

Counted Thread Embroidery, by James Norbury (out of print).

Florentine Embroidery, by Barbara Snook. New York: Crown Publishers, Inc.

Encyclopedia of Needlework, by Thérèse de Dillmont. France: Mullhouse. (p. 232 to 235, illustration facind p. 720)

Canvas Work and Design, by Jennifer Gray. London: B. T. Batsford Ltd. (many illustrations)

Bargello, Florentine Canvas Work, by Elsa Williams. New York: Van Nostrand-Reinhold Company.

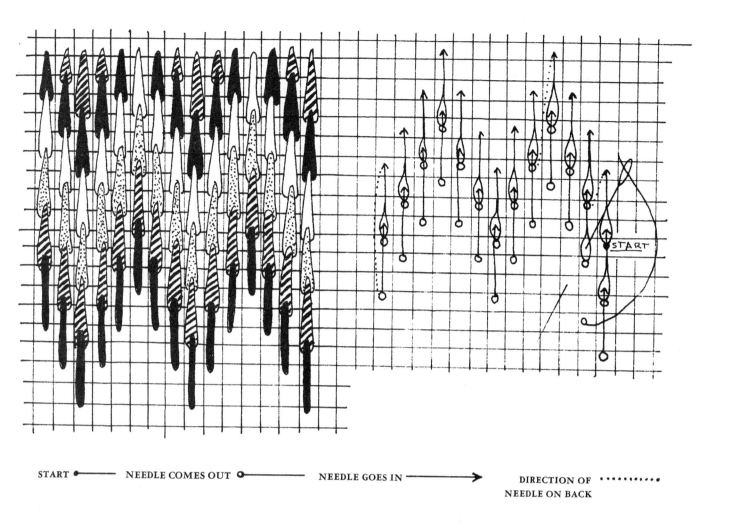

START •——— NEEDLE COMES OUT o———— NEEDLE GOES IN ———————▶ DIRECTION OF •••••••••••
NEEDLE ON BACK

SPLIT FLORENTINE

Make a row in regular Florentine (p. 12) in whatever design you wish. Each stitch should cover 4 horizontal threads. Start second row 3 threads down and insert needle through bottoms of stitches of first row, encroaching over bottom canvas thread. Make all succeeding rows in this manner.

The diagram at left shows compensating stitches at top. You will have to do these compensating stitches first, and then proceed with regular pattern.

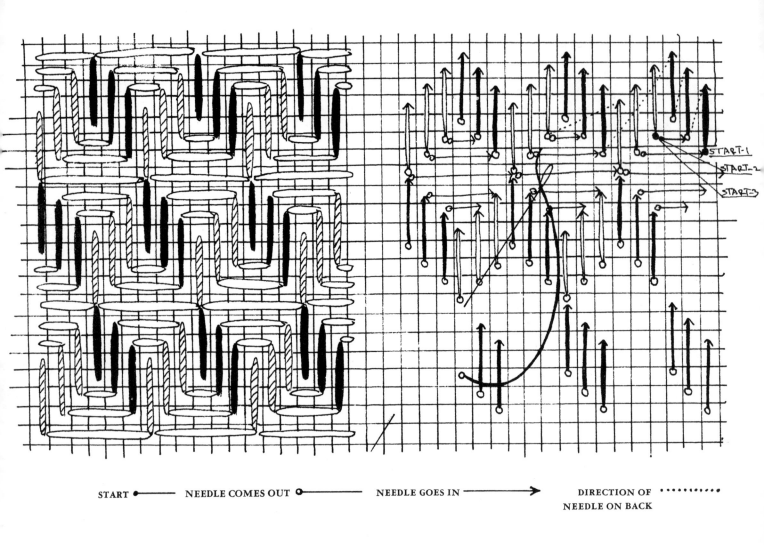

START ●————— NEEDLE COMES OUT ○————— NEEDLE GOES IN ⟶ DIRECTION OF ··········· NEEDLE ON BACK

FLORENTINE & SATIN

Work zigzag rows of Florentine (p. 12), alternating 2 values of 1 color. Have the top points of second row meet bottom points of first row, leaving a diagonal square. Cover the square with horizontal stitches, using a lighter value of the same color. If you wish to finish with 1 shade before starting another, be sure to locate stitches properly.

This stitch pattern creates the illusion of stacked cubes.

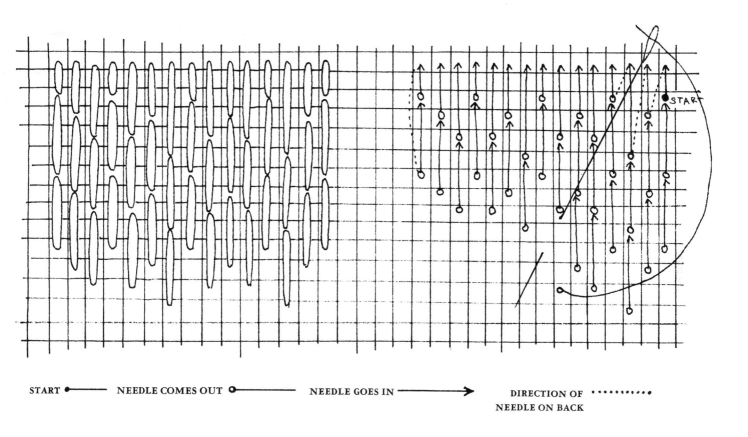

START ●——— NEEDLE COMES OUT ○———————— NEEDLE GOES IN ————————▶ DIRECTION OF ·········
NEEDLE ON BACK

HIT-A-MISS FLORENTINE

Make the first row of stitches, covering from 2 to 5 threads. Use no special sequence, just "hit-a-miss." Subsequent rows are then made of stitches covering 4 threads, and following the uneven line made by the ends of stitches of first row. You may further vary the length of the stitches if you wish. The object is to achieve an allover effect with no pattern.

This stitch pattern is similar in principle to Long and Short in surface stitchery. You may use the split stitch principle if you wish. It can be shaded, and is good for background.

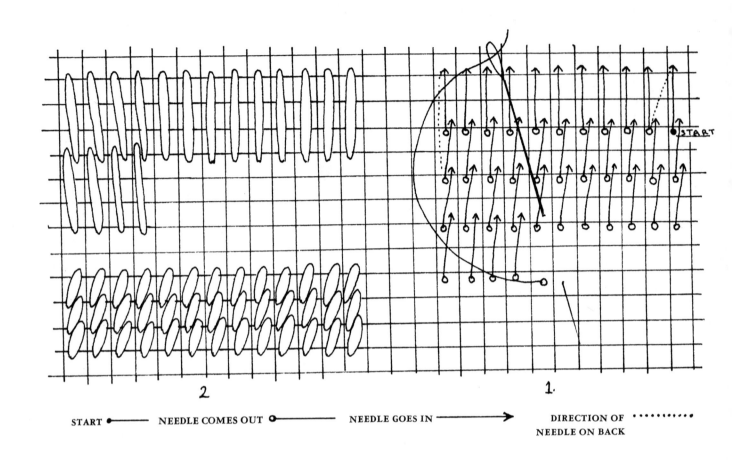

2   **1.**

ENCROACHED GOBELIN 1

All stitches are vertical, made over 2, 3, 4, or more horizontal threads. In diagram 1 the stitches cover 3 threads. The second row is made 2 threads down and encroaches over 1 thread of first row. Because the stitches of the second row push the bottoms of first row stitches aside, they appear to be slanting, but they are worked vertically. You may encroach on either the left or the right side of stitches of first row, but once you have chosen a side, stick with it. This is a good simple background stitch as it covers the canvas well. It is also good for shading.

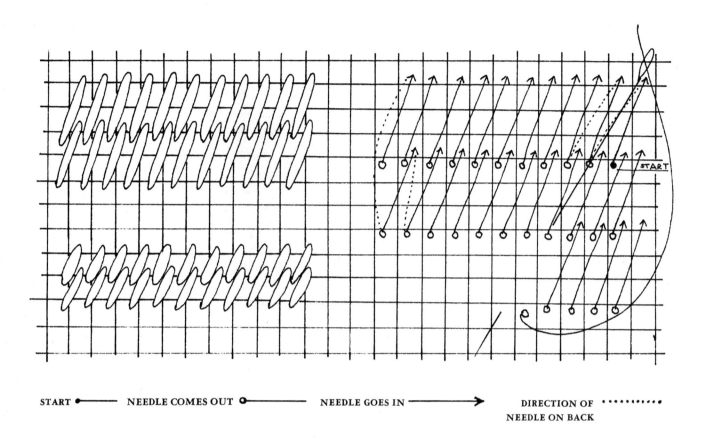

START ●——— NEEDLE COMES OUT ○————— NEEDLE GOES IN ——————▶ DIRECTION OF ·········
NEEDLE ON BACK

ENCROACHED GOBELIN 2

The number of horizontal threads in this slanting version of Encroached Gobelin may vary, but stitches cover only 1 vertical thread. In the diagram at the right the stitches are made over 4 horizontal and 1 vertical threads. You may encroach on either the left or right sides of bottoms of stitches of first row, but once you have chosen a side, stick with it. You will note that the first stitch of second row encroaches over the next to last stitch of first row. This is a good simple background stitch as it covers the canvas well. It is also good for shading.

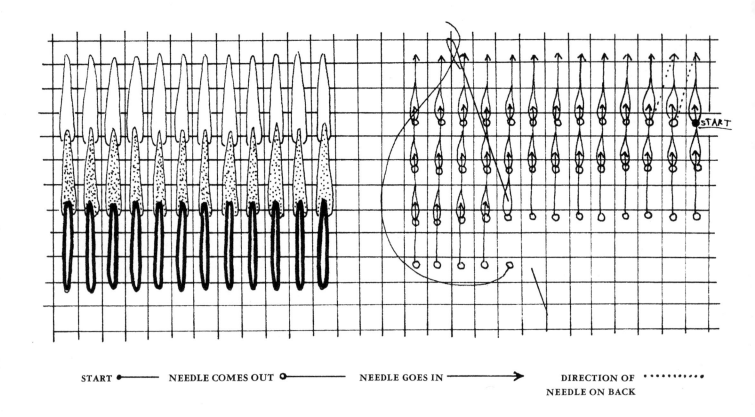

START ●━━━━ NEEDLE COMES OUT ○━━━━ NEEDLE GOES IN ━━━━━━▶ DIRECTION OF ••••••••••
                                                            NEEDLE ON BACK

SPLIT ENCROACHED GOBELIN

Make a row of straight Encroached Gobelin stitches (p. 16), covering as many horizontal threads as you desire. In the second row insert the needle through the bottoms of the stitches in row 1, overlapping 1 canvas thread. In the second and succeeding rows, 1 less thread is covered than in row 1. Bottom thread in row 1 serves 2 rows. This stitch covers canvas well and is good for shading. This principle can be applied to many upright stitches, but is not recommended where it would interfere with a definite stitch pattern, e.g., Hungarian (p. 8) or Hungarian Ground (p. 19).

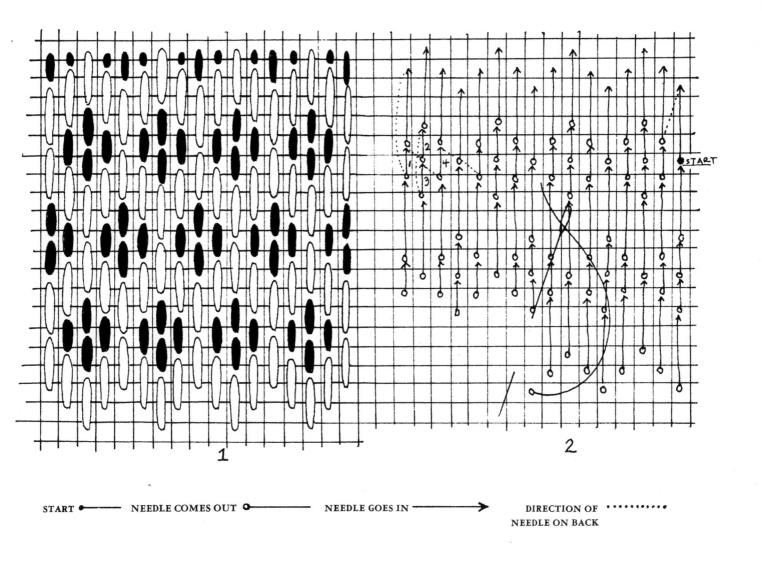

START ●━━━━ NEEDLE COMES OUT ○━━━━ NEEDLE GOES IN ━━━━▶ DIRECTION OF ●●●●●●●●●●
NEEDLE ON BACK

HUNGARIAN GROUND

All one color. Make a zigzag of vertical stitches, each over 3 or 4 threads. The second and third stitches are 1 and 2 threads higher than the first stitch. The fourth and fifth stitches step down again so the fifth stitch is even with the first. Continue across the row in this manner. Work second row from left to right, making groups of 4 small stitches. Follow the numbered sequence in the diagram. The third row is like the first except that the direction of the points is reversed. The fourth row is like the second, etc. If you wish, you may substitute a Hungarian stitch unit (p. 8) (3 stitches, over 2 threads, 4 threads, 2 threads) in place of the 4 short stitch groups in rows 2, 4, etc.

Two colors. Work rows 1, 3, 5, etc., first in 1 color, and then fill in 2, 4, etc., with the 4 short stitches or Hungarian stitch units in a contrasting color.

Diagram 1 shows the stitch pattern done in two colors using the Hungarian stitch units for rows 2 and 4. Diagram 2 shows the stitch pattern done in one color using the 4 short stitch units. There is a compensating row at the top of diagram 1.

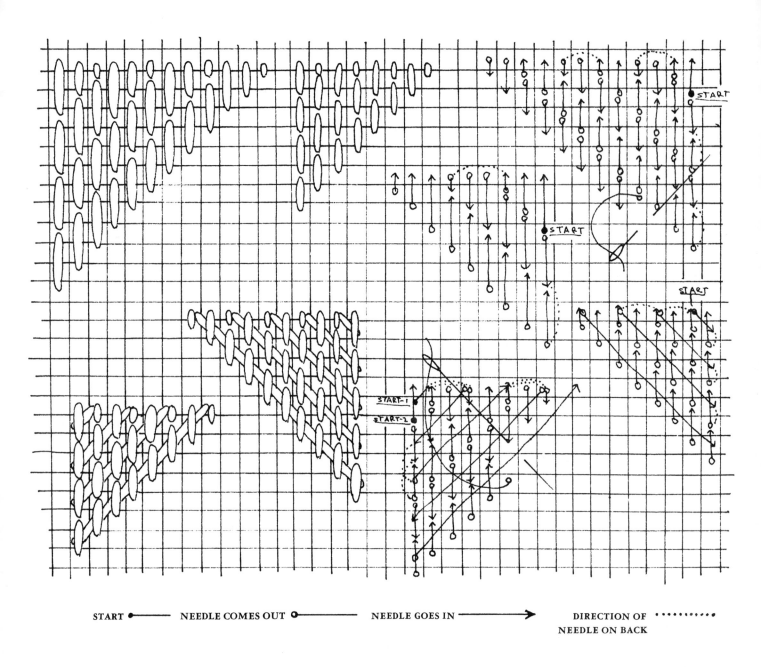

START ●———— NEEDLE COMES OUT ○———— NEEDLE GOES IN ————→ DIRECTION OF ···········
NEEDLE ON BACK

DIAGONAL GOBELIN

The stitches are straight but the rows are diagonal. Each stitch covers 2 or more horizontal threads and, if it is used, a padding strand. Don't pull yarn too tight or canvas will peep. This stitch pattern can be used in combination with Straight Gobelin (p. 1). In the plain version the rows alternate in direction. In the padded versions they alternate if the padding is a separate strand. The rows are all worked from top to bottom if the working strand is used for padding. The diagrams show compensation for straight edges. The stitch looks like a small size Bricking stitch (p. 2), but is produced differently. Rows may slant in either direction. For diagonal rows slanting from upper right to lower left, start in upper left corner.

20

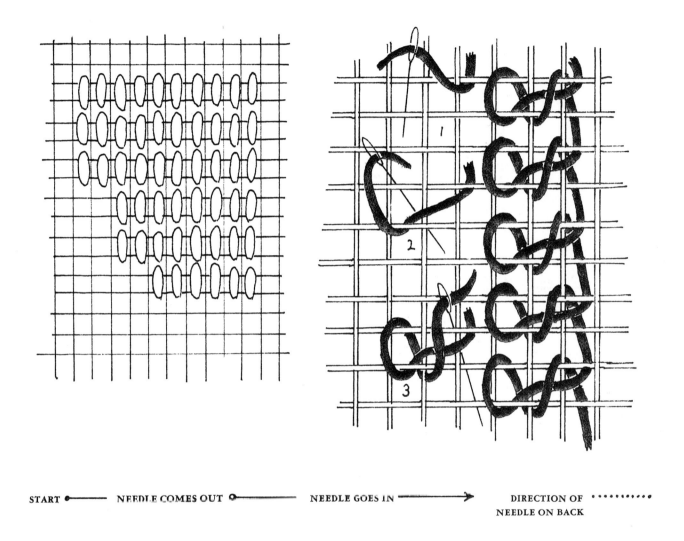

START ●————— NEEDLE COMES OUT ○————— NEEDLE GOES IN ⟶ DIRECTION OF • • • • • • • • • •
NEEDLE ON BACK

RENAISSANCE

Follow the steps in the diagram. Work in double vertical rows, starting each row at the top. The effect is the same as Straight Gobelin (p. 1).

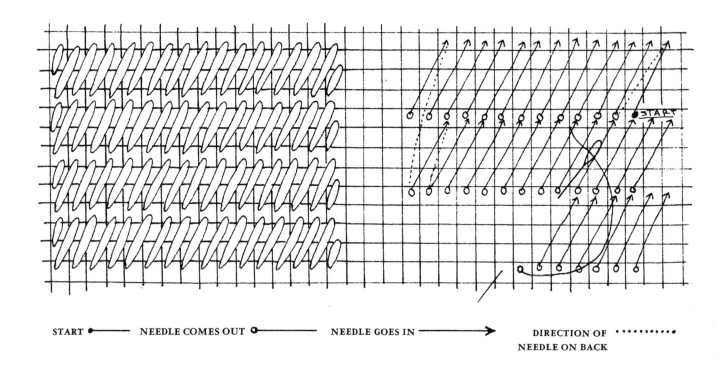

START ●————— NEEDLE COMES OUT ○————— NEEDLE GOES IN ————————▶ DIRECTION OF · · · · · · · · · ·
NEEDLE ON BACK

SLANTED GOBELIN

The number of horizontal threads covered and the degree of slant may be varied. The diagrams show two different counts. Work parallel stitches in horizontal rows, using every hole. The diagram at left shows compensating stitches along the sides. One row makes an attractive stripe, especially if worked on the true diagonal.

Note: Unless you put your canvas on a frame before beginning to work, you should not cover large areas with this stitch, because it distorts the canvas badly. This can be avoided by alternating the slant of the rows, as in Knitting 2 (p. 112).

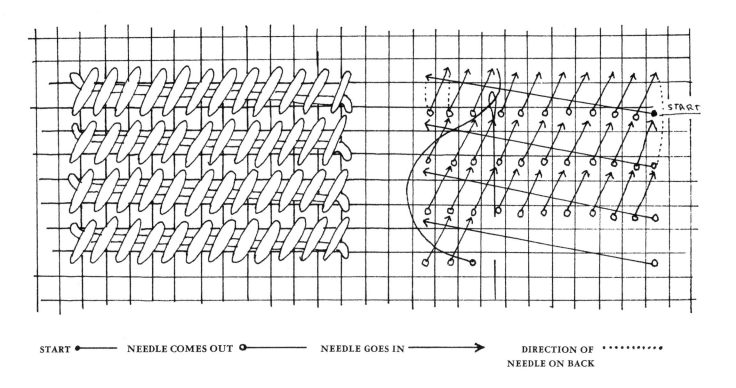

START ●━━━ NEEDLE COMES OUT ○━━━ NEEDLE GOES IN ━━━━▶ DIRECTION OF • • • • • • • • • •
NEEDLE ON BACK

PADDED SATIN*

This is a padded Slanted Gobelin stitch. A strand is laid, right to left, over 2 horizontal threads, and as many vertical threads as the row requires. Needle emerges 2 threads below end of laid strand. Covering stitches are made over 2 horizontal and 1 vertical threads, using every hole. Needle goes under 2 horizontal threads, and the stitches are worked from left to right. For second row laid strand begins 2 threads below beginning of laid strand of row 1.

* Left-handed people reverse "left" and "right."

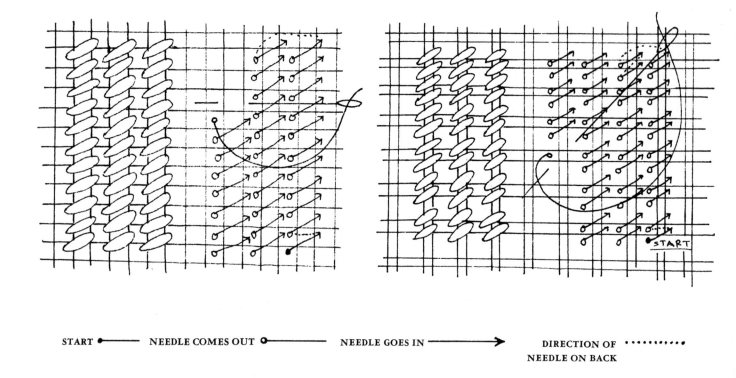

START ●————— NEEDLE COMES OUT ⊙———————— NEEDLE GOES IN ————————▶ DIRECTION OF ··········● NEEDLE ON BACK

REP*

This can be worked on double or single mesh canvas. Work in vertical rows.

On double mesh canvas stitches cover both vertical threads in group, but only 1 horizontal thread of group. The stitch pattern produces a corded effect.

On single mesh canvas stitches cover 1 horizontal and 2 vertical threads. On the ascending row the needle passes under 2 vertical threads. On the descending row the needle passes under 2 intersections, down, left. Viewed from the side this stitch pattern resembles a small size Slanted Gobelin (p. 22).

* Left-handed people reverse "left" and "right."

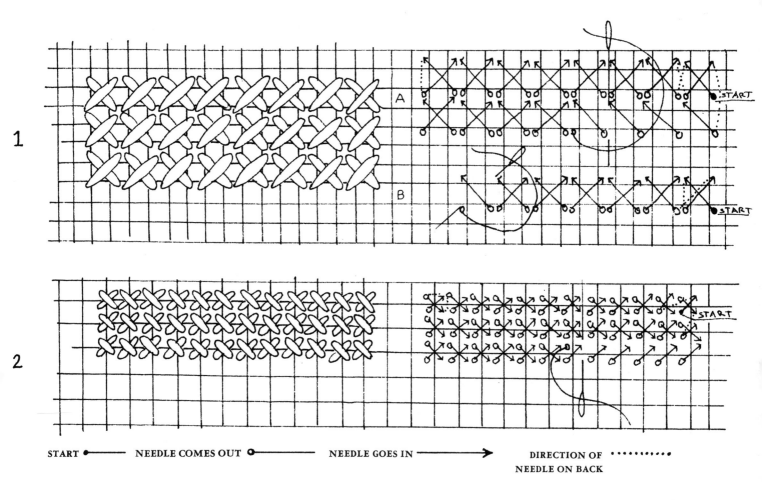

START ●————— NEEDLE COMES OUT ○————— NEEDLE GOES IN ————→ DIRECTION OF ··········
NEEDLE ON BACK

DIAGONAL CROSS*
Cross Stitch (Gros Point and Petit Point)

1. This stitch pattern can be produced two ways. Half of the cross can be worked across row and completed on return journey (A), or you can complete each cross as you go along (B). Remember to keep the same stitch on top of all crosses.

2. The first half of the cross is made in Horizontal or Continental Tent 2 (p. 89), the needle passing under 2 vertical and 1 horizontal threads. Work from right to left. Complete the crosses with Half Cross Tent 1 stitch (p. 88) pointing in the opposite direction. The Half Cross Tent stitch cannot be used alone on single mesh canvas but the back of the Horizontal or Continental stitches holds these stitches in place. Unless fairly fine yarn is used, this stitch pattern will look like a Tent stitch, as the underneath stitches will not show. They give added wearing quality, however, and prevent the distortion of the canvas. On double mesh canvas the small Diagonal Cross stitch can be worked like the large size.

The French words, *Gros Point* and *Petit Point,* which mean "large stitch" and "small stitch," are erroneously applied to the large and small Tent stitch made on double mesh canvas. The terms are very old and apply to the Diagonal Cross stitch.

* Left-handed people reverse "left" and "right."

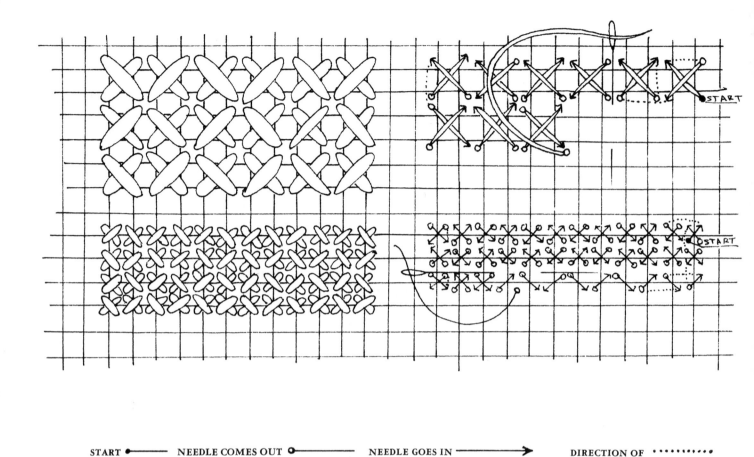

START •———— NEEDLE COMES OUT ○———— NEEDLE GOES IN ————————▶ DIRECTION OF • • • • • • • • • •
NEEDLE ON BACK

CROSS-STITCH-GONE-WRONG*

Diagonal Cross stitch (p. 25) is usually made with the same stitch on top over the entire area. This stitch pattern deliberately reverses the top stitch on every other cross.

1. Large size. Work Diagonal Cross stitches in horizontal rows over 2 intersections each way, completing each cross as you go along. By passing the needle under 2 threads, vertically or horizontally each time, the stitches on top of the crosses will alternate in direction. A pattern of squares is formed on the back.

2. Small size. Make a diagonal stitch over 1 intersection up, right. Pass the needle under 2 vertical threads to the left. Now insert the needle over 1 intersection down, right, and pass the needle under 2 vertical threads to the left again. Continue across the row in this manner, making a zigzag of half crosses. Pass the needle under 1 thread to begin completing crosses on return journey, passing needle under 2 threads each time. Make the first stitch of second row in the *same* direction as last stitch of return journey of row 1, so that the completing stitch will be in the opposite direction.

* Left-handed people reverse "left" and "right."

26

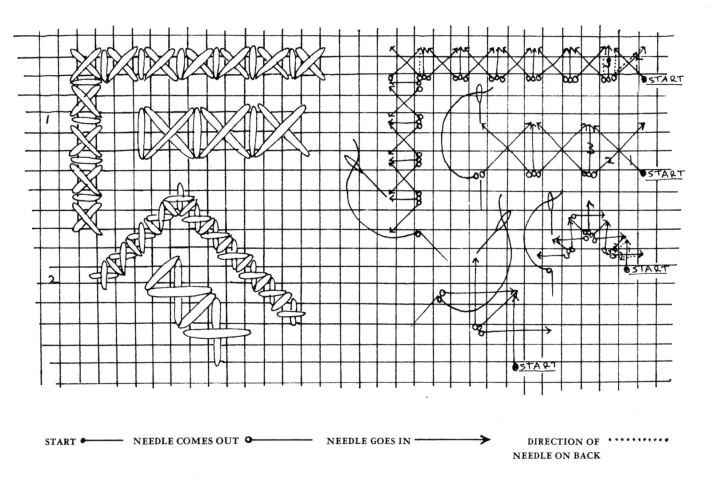

START ● —— NEEDLE COMES OUT ○—— NEEDLE GOES IN ——→ DIRECTION OF ⋯⋯⋯•
NEEDLE ON BACK

CROSS STITCH WITH BAR 1 & 2*

1. Straight. Work cross stitches over 2 or 3 intersections and place straight stitches between them. When turning corner be careful to place bars only between crosses, not at end.

2. Diagonal. The diagonal form is slightly smaller than the straight but equally effective. Work a Straight Cross (p. 31) over 2 or 4 (you can't use 3) threads each way, and then a diagonal bar over 1 or 2 intersections.

This is a very versatile stitch. It can be worked vertically, horizontally, or diagonally, and turns corners easily. It is good for stems, striping, or edging. If worked with fairly heavy yarn, it loses its identity as a cross stitch pattern, but produces a nubby, textured rounded row which contrasts well with smooth stitches such as padded Straight Gobelin (p. 1).

* Left-handed people reverse "left" and "right."

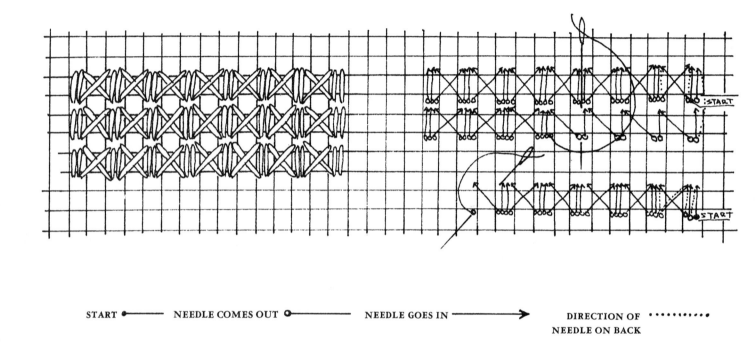

START ●——— NEEDLE COMES OUT ○——— NEEDLE GOES IN ———⟶ DIRECTION OF ⋯⋯⋯⋯
NEEDLE ON BACK

ZIGZAG

Starting at the right, work 1 vertical stitch over 2 threads, bringing the needle out at beginning of stitch. Then make a diagonal stitch over 2 intersections up, left. Bring needle out 2 threads down. Continue across the row with 1 vertical and 1 diagonal stitch. At the end of the row make 2 vertical stitches. Then complete crosses and add a second vertical stitch on return journey. The needle goes under 2 threads for all stitches.

It is possible to work this stitch pattern complete in 1 journey. Work like Cross with Bar (p. 27), but add an extra bar.

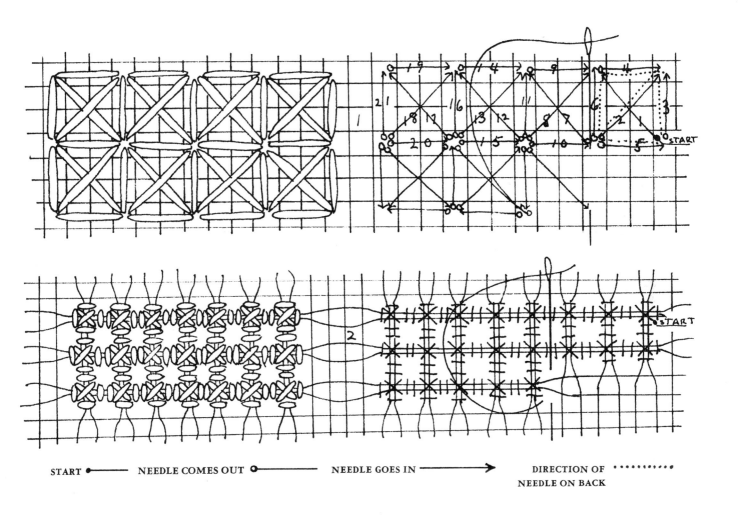

ITALIAN CROSS 1 & 2

Italian Cross 1. Work diagonal cross stitches over 2, 3, or 4 intersections and, as you go along, put vertical and horizontal stitches between them. Be careful to keep the top stitches of crosses going in the same direction.

Italian Cross 2. This form of Italian Cross is worked over 2 intersections and 2 threads each way. Use fine yarn and pull it tight to make the holes. Follow the sequence of stitches illustrated in diagram for Italian Cross 1. Add an extra stitch between crosses. It may be necessary to add a third vertical or horizontal stitch between crosses to be sure to cover the canvas threads well. Be careful to have tension-pull stitches in the right direction. In the second row the horizontal stitch above the cross added to the one worked in the first row will balance the vertical stitches between cross stitches.

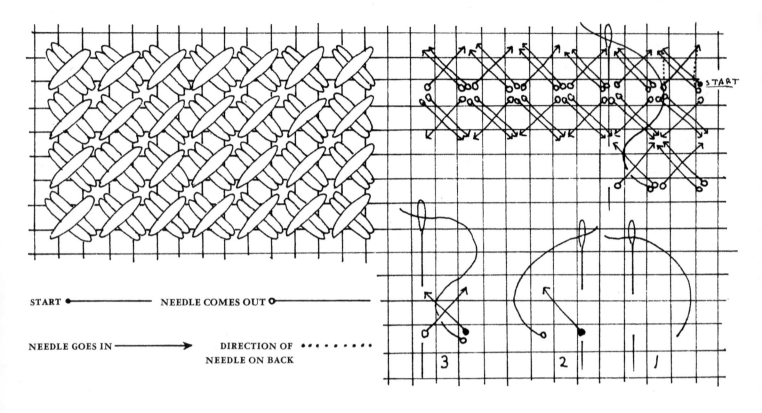

START ●———————— NEEDLE COMES OUT ⊙——————————

NEEDLE GOES IN ————————▶   DIRECTION OF ● ● ● ● ● ● ● ●
                             NEEDLE ON BACK

REINFORCED CROSS

Make a regular Diagonal Cross stitch (p. 25) over 2 threads each way. Bring needle out at same place as start of first stitch. Slip the needle under second stitch, insert it in upper left corner, and bring it out 2 threads down for beginning of next stitch pattern. This makes 2 stitches from lower right to upper left and 1 stitch from lower left to upper right. Sometimes the reinforcing stitch lies on top of the first stitch but it usually lies beside it.

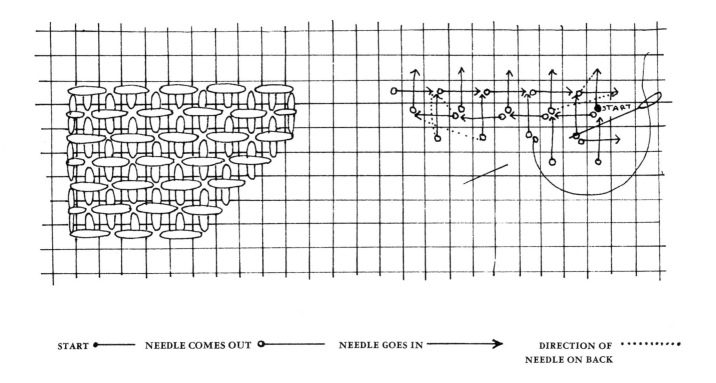

STRAIGHT CROSS

This stitch is worked over 2 horizontal and then 2 vertical threads. Complete each cross as you go along. In the second row the crosses fit up between those of first row; the tops of the vertical stitches using the same holes as the horizontal stitches of first row, and the sides using the same holes as bottoms of first row stitches. In the right diagram you will notice in the first row the horizontal stitches point to the right, that is, the needle comes out at the left and goes in at the right. In the second row this is reversed. This is done to give the crosses a high nubby look, which would be uniform on all rows. Turn work one-fourth way around and work second row vertically.

Compensation for straight edges is shown in the left diagram. This is achieved by working one part of the cross over only 1 thread. Always keep the horizontal stitch on top. No compensation is needed for diagonal edges.

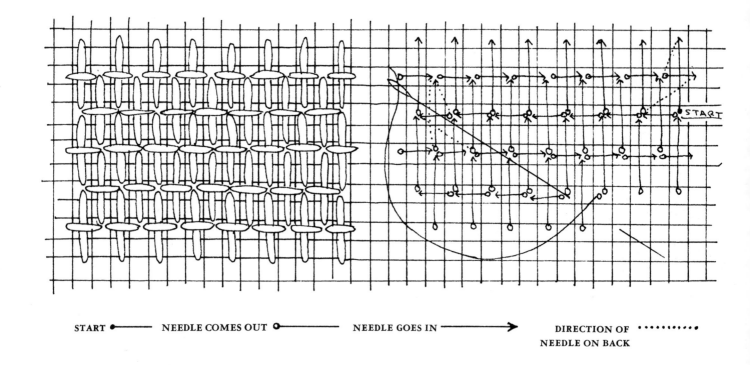

START •——— NEEDLE COMES OUT ○——— NEEDLE GOES IN ——————▶ DIRECTION OF •••••••••
NEEDLE ON BACK

STRAIGHT CROSS VARIATION

Make a vertical stitch over 4 threads, and bring the needle out 2 threads down and 1 thread to the left. Insert the needle 2 threads to the right, and over the first stitch. Bring the needle out 2 threads to the left of the beginning of first stitch for next vertical stitch. Continue across the row in this manner.

In the second row the crosses fit up between crosses of first row, using the same holes as the sides and bottoms of crosses of first row. The short horizontal stitches of the second row start at the right side so they will be raised, and uniform with the first row.

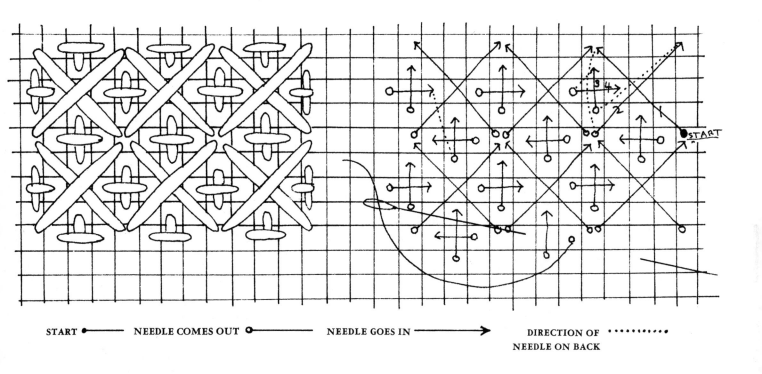

LARGE CROSS WITH STRAIGHT CROSS

Work large diagonal crosses over 4 intersections with straight crosses between them. Complete each unit as you go along. The return or second row is all straight crosses worked between and below legs of large crosses. The third row is like the first, the fourth like the second, etc. The diagram at the left shows compensation for straight edges. The straight cross can be worked in a contrasting color.

33

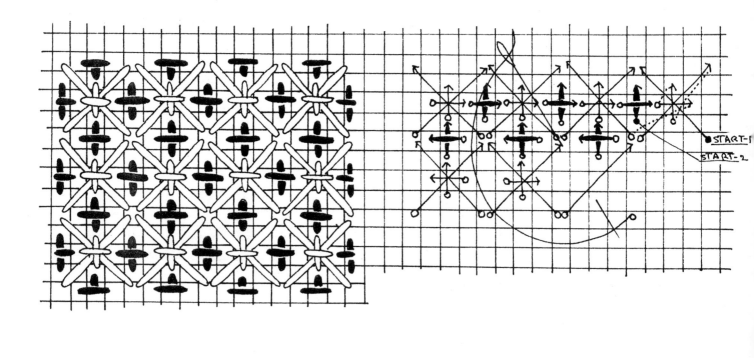

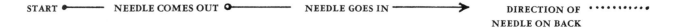

START ●————— NEEDLE COMES OUT ○————— NEEDLE GOES IN ————→ DIRECTION OF ·········•
NEEDLE ON BACK

LARGE CROSS WITH STRAIGHT CROSS VARIATION

Step 1. Work a row of large diagonal crosses, over 4 intersections each way, with small straight crosses over their intersecting arms, starting at right. In second row work this combination from left to right so arms of large crosses meet. Cover entire area in this manner.

Step 2. With a contrasting color, work Straight Crosses (p. 31) between large crosses of first row, starting at right. The second row of Straight Crosses is worked between large crosses of first and second row, left to right. Then the third row is worked between large crosses of second row, as in row 1.

Because of the conflicting directions of the rows, it is best to finish step 1 before starting step 2.
The diagram at left shows compensation for straight edges.

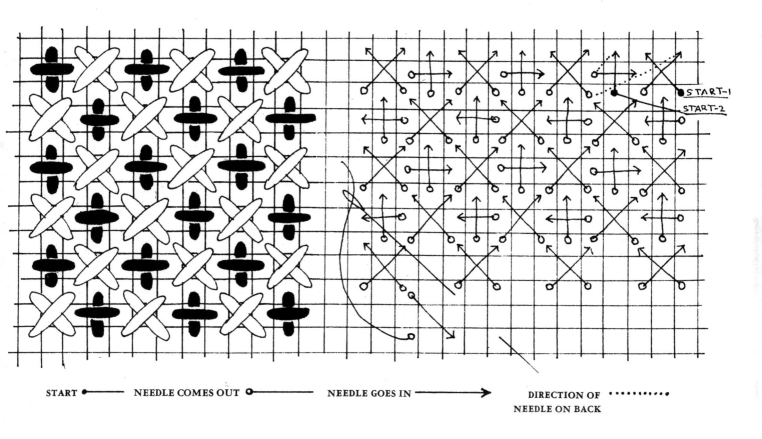

START ●——— NEEDLE COMES OUT ○——— NEEDLE GOES IN ———→ DIRECTION OF ••••••••••••
NEEDLE ON BACK

ST. GEORGE & ST. ANDREW

Step 1. Work diagonal crosses (St. Andrew's cross) over 2 intersections each way, leaving 2 threads between crosses. In the second row work crosses diagonally down from those of first row, forming a checker pattern. As in regular Diagonal Cross stitch, work half of the crosses from right to left and complete on the return journey.

Step 2. In the spaces left between diagonal crosses work straight crosses (St. George's cross) in a contrasting color. Complete each cross before starting the next one.

Heavy yarn is needed to cover canvas.

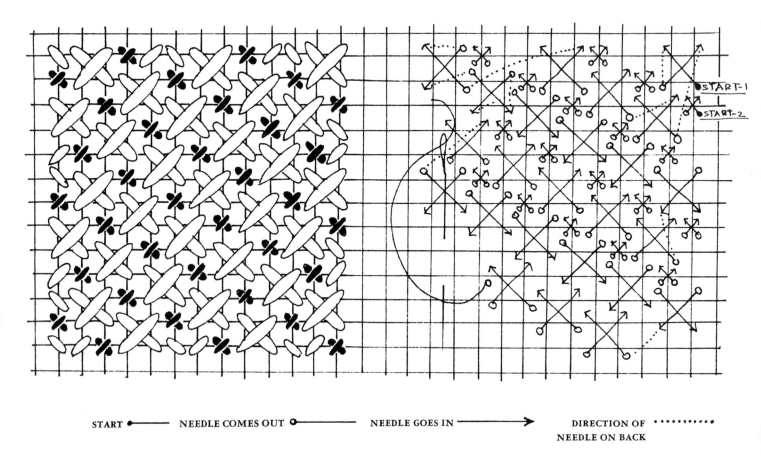

START ●——— NEEDLE COMES OUT ○——— NEEDLE GOES IN ——→ DIRECTION OF ·········•
NEEDLE ON BACK

STAGGERED CROSS

This cross-stitch pattern differs from the conventional pattern in that the crosses are not in rows beside and below each other. The rows slant gradually, 1 horizontal thread at a time, down to the right. Instead of being directly under each other, the rows slant 1 vertical thread to the left for each cross. This leaves evenly spaced canvas intersections, which are covered with small crosses in a contrasting color.

Because of the direction of the rows, compensation is rather difficult. Don't attempt to start at a horizontal edge. Work across a large area, and then work to the bottom of the area to be covered. Turn work halfway around (top at bottom), and, fitting a row up to your first row, work to the bottom again. The diagram at left shows compensation for straight edges.

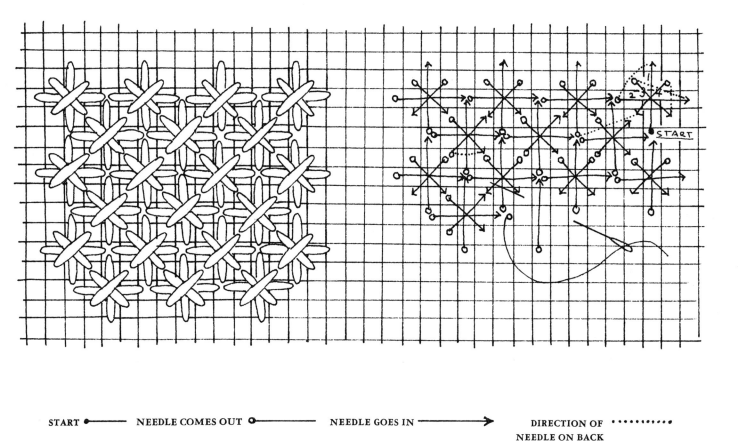

DOUBLE STRAIGHT CROSS

Work a large straight cross, over 4 threads each way, and then a smaller diagonal cross stitch over 2 intersections each way on top. In the second row the units fit up between those of the first row, the tops of the large straight crosses using the same holes as the horizontal stitches of the first row. This stitch pattern produces a high diamond-shaped square. If the alternating rows are done in contrasting colors, it makes a diagonal checkerboard.

Another interesting variation is achieved by making the large straight cross in one shade, and the smaller diagonal cross in a lighter shade of the same color. Compensating for straight vertical or horizontal edges is possible, but the effect of this pattern is best maintained by fitting the units against diagonal lines, or using other patterns to fill the edges; for example half a Hungarian unit (p. 8).

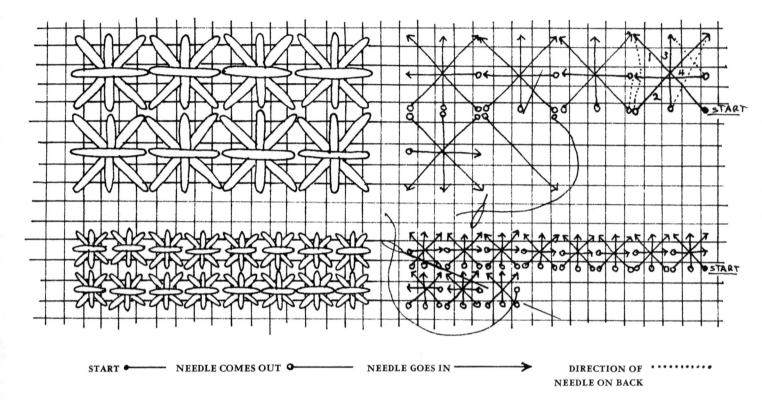

START ●———— NEEDLE COMES OUT ○———— NEEDLE GOES IN ————→ DIRECTION OF ·········
                                                          NEEDLE ON BACK

SMYRNA CROSS
Double Cross

Work a large diagonal cross stitch over 4 intersections each way, and then a large straight cross stitch, covering 4 threads each way over it. Be sure the top stitches of the straight crosses are either all vertical or all horizontal. Back stitches between units may be needed to cover the canvas.

The small version is worked over 2 threads each way. If it is worked with fairly heavy yarn, it makes a high squared mound.

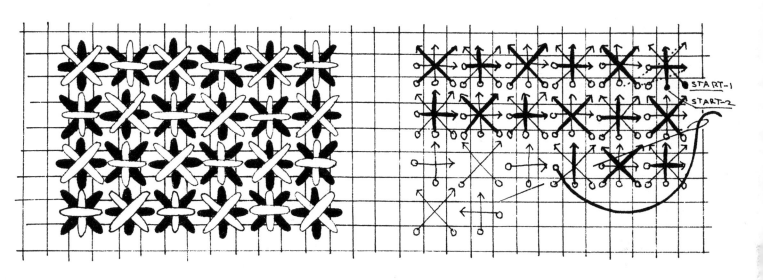

REVERSED DOUBLE CROSS

Work diagonal and straight crosses covering 2 threads each way alternately across row. Second row has straight crosses below diagonal ones and vice versa. With contrasting yarn complete double crosses, diagonal over straight, and straight over diagonal. This stitch pattern can be worked over 4 threads instead of 2.

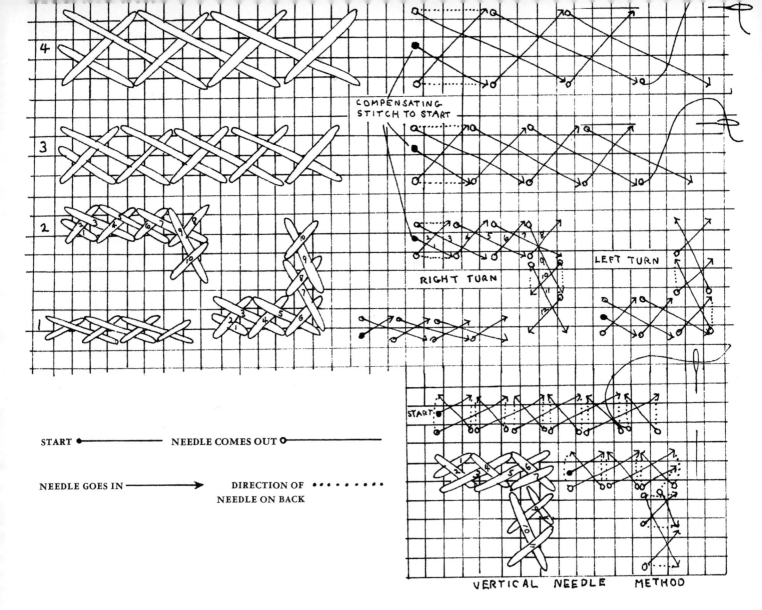

LONG-LEGGED CROSS*
Greek Cross

4. So as to avoid an empty place where canvas would show, start with a compensating stitch at left end. Bring needle out 2 threads down from top of area to be covered. Insert needle 4 threads to right and 2 threads down. Bring needle out 4 threads to left. Now make first regular stitch up, right, over the 4 intersections. Pass needle under 4 threads to left. Insert needle 4 threads to right of end of compensating stitch for long leg. Continue across row, inserting needle 4 threads to right of ends of previous stitches at top and bottom of row. There will be 2 lines of stitches, top and bottom, on the back. Heavy yarn will be needed to cover canvas.

3. The compensating stitch is made 1 thread down from the top at left end of row. Follow the directions for the 4 thread form, using units of 3 instead of 4. This size is about the same as large Diagonal Long-Legged Cross (p. 41).

2. This is made the same way, using units of 2. The diagrams for this form show how to turn left and right corners. Follow numbers in diagrams. After turning corners, turn canvas one-quarter way around, and continue as in beginning, before turn.

1. This form has units 2 threads wide, but only 1 thread high. No compensating stitch is needed.

All 4 forms can be used to cover an area. For second row, turn work halfway around and proceed as in first row.

* Left-handed people reverse "left" and "right."

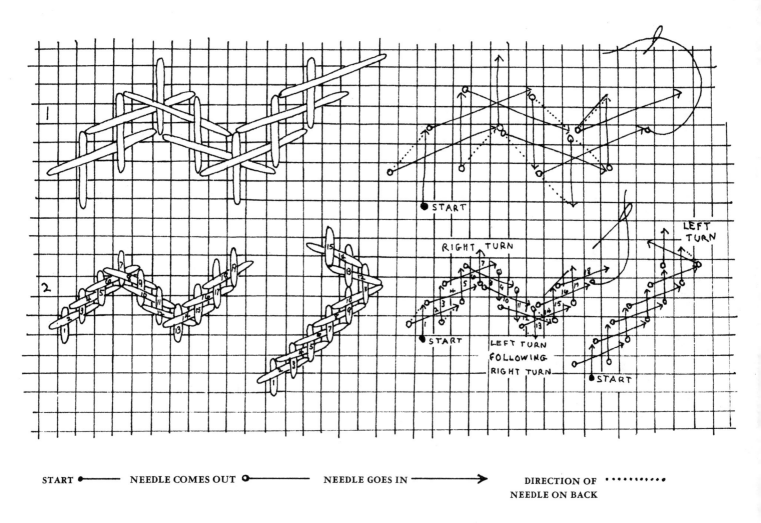

START •————— NEEDLE COMES OUT o—————— NEEDLE GOES IN ————→ DIRECTION OF • • • • • • • • •
                                                              NEEDLE ON BACK

DIAGONAL LONG-LEGGED CROSS*

1. Begin with a vertical stitch up over 4 threads. Bring needle out 2 intersections down, left. Insert needle 4 threads to right of top of first stitch and bring it out 2 intersections down, left. Repeat these 2 stitches. The row of stitches will progress diagonally up, right.

   Right turn. Make the vertical stitch. The long stitch starts in the same place but needle is inserted 4 threads to right of *bottom* of vertical stitch. Bring needle out 2 intersections up, left. The vertical stitch is now made from top to bottom, the needle passing under 2 intersections up, left, each time. The row of stitches will now progress diagonally down, right. There will be two rows of diagonal stitches on the back of your work.

   Left turn. Make the vertical stitch. Bring the needle out at the end of the last long stitch. Make a long stitch up, left, inserting the needle 4 threads to left of end of last vertical stitch. Make subsequent stitches with needle passing under 2 intersections down, right. Follow these directions for left and right turns for small size, but make everything half size.

   Left turn following right turn and right turn following left turn are different from these directions. See diagrams. Always start turns after short stitch.

2. The small version is worked the same as the large, but everything is half size. Both forms can be used to cover an area. Turn work halfway around for second row and proceed as in first row.

* Left-handed people reverse "left" and "right."

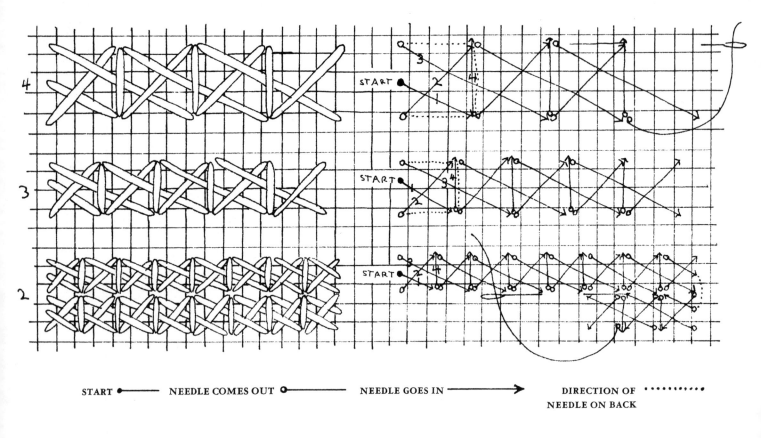

START ●——— NEEDLE COMES OUT ⊙——— NEEDLE GOES IN ———→ DIRECTION OF ∙∙∙∙∙∙∙∙∙∙∙
NEEDLE ON BACK

MONTENEGRIN*

Begin at left with a compensating stitch as in Long-Legged Cross, then make a stitch covering 4 (3, 2) intersections, up, right. Bring needle out 4 (3, 2) threads to left. The long stitch covers 4 (3, 2) horizontal and 8 (6, 4) vertical threads, down, right. Again bring needle out 4 (3, 2) threads to left. Make a vertical stitch covering 4 (3, 2) threads and bring needle out where stitch began. Do not invert canvas for second row. Reverse the "right" and "left" of directions for first row.

* Left-handed people reverse "left" and "right."

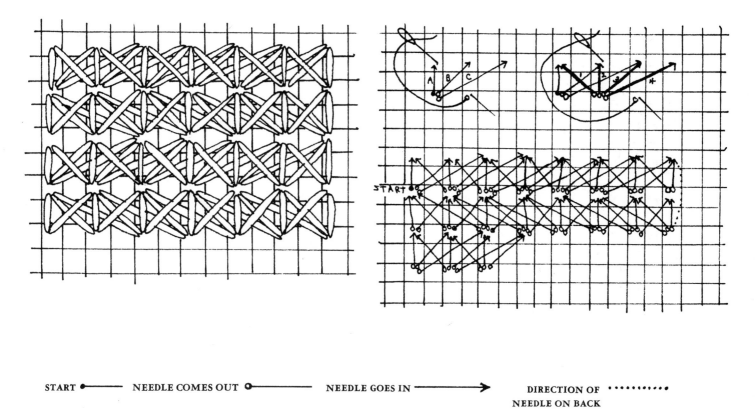

MONTENEGRIN VARIATION

This looks like Cross Stich with Bar (p. 27) with an added long slanting stitch, but the progression of stitches is different. Follow steps in diagrams. Work A, B, and C in diagram 1. Then, 2 threads to the right, do steps 1, 2, 3, 4 in diagram 2.

Repeat steps 1, 2, 3, and 4 two threads to the right each time. At the end of the row omit step 4 and add steps 1 and 2.

For the second row begin again with A, B, and C reversing the "right" and "left" of directions for row 1.

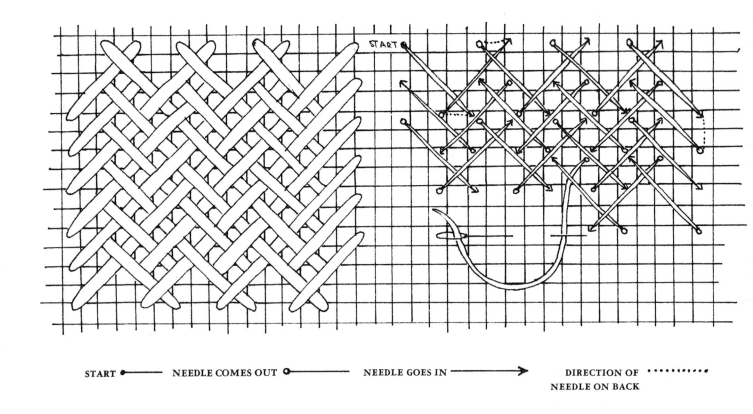

START ●—— NEEDLE COMES OUT ⊶—— NEEDLE GOES IN ——→ DIRECTION OF •••••••••
NEEDLE ON BACK

HERRINGBONE*

Method 1. Row 1 (left to right). The first stitch is made over 4 intersections diagonally down, right. Bring needle out 2 threads to left. The second stitch goes diagonally up, right, over 4 intersections. Bring needle out 2 threads to left. Repeat these 2 stitches to end of row.

Row 2 (right to left). The second row starts 2 threads below end of first row. The stitches parallel those of first row with needle position reversed. In order to produce the same overlap of stitches as in row 1, it is necessary to pass needle under completed stitch before pulling it tight. See diagram. The third row is like the first; the fourth like the second, etc.

Method 2. This is simpler but more inconvenient. You start every row at the left. The number of horizontal threads covered may be varied but not the number of vertical ones.

* Left-handed people reverse "left" and "right."

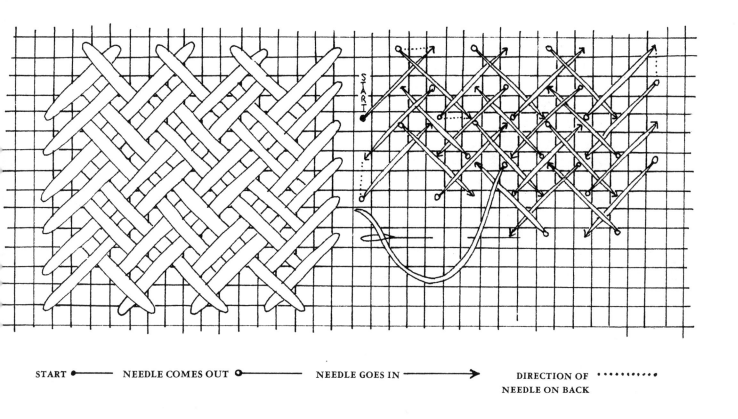

HERRINGBONE-GONE-WRONG*

True Herringbone (p. 44) has the same overlap of stitches in all rows. If the rows are made alternately from left to right and then from right to left a reverse of overlap is obtained. This is Herringbone-Gone-Wrong. The difference seems slight, but the effect obtained is quite different. Simply work Herringbone stitch back and forth, dropping down 2 threads each row.

* Left-handed people reverse "left" and "right."

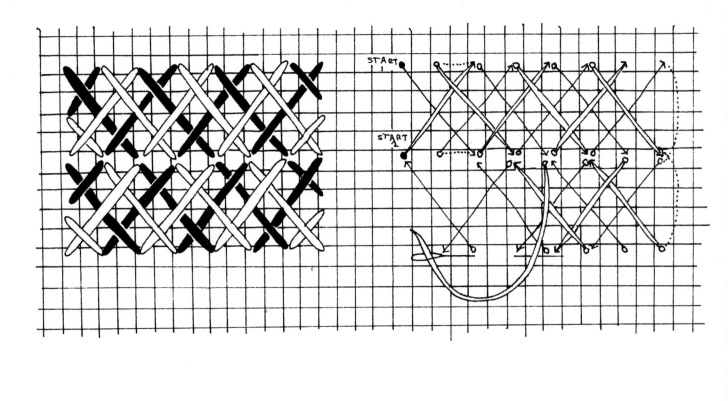

START ●——— NEEDLE COMES OUT ○——— NEEDLE GOES IN ——————▶ DIRECTION OF ••••••••••
NEEDLE ON BACK

DOUBLE HERRINGBONE*

Step 1. Work a row of Herringbone (p. 44) in the usual way, covering 4 or more horizontal threads but only 4 vertical threads. This number cannot vary. Begin at left. Second row starts the same number of horizontal threads down as you covered in first row. There is no overlapping of rows.

Step 2. Start 2 threads to left of bottom of second stitch of first row, directly below start of step 1. Make stitches like those in step 1, filling in spaces. Contrasting colors are effective. Diagram at left shows compensating stitches at ends of rows.

* Left-handed people reverse "left" and "right."

46

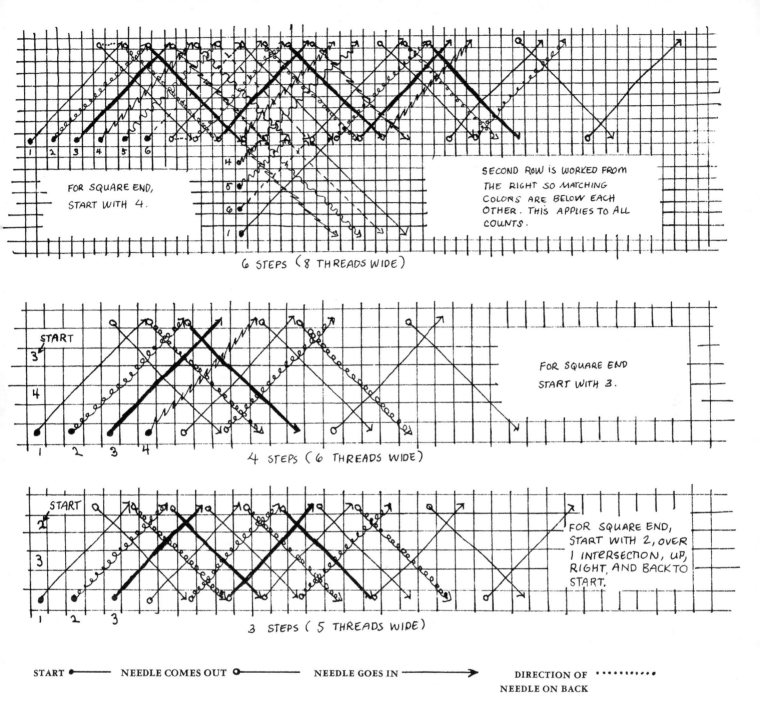

FOR SQUARE END,
START WITH 4.

SECOND ROW IS WORKED FROM
THE RIGHT SO MATCHING
COLORS ARE BELOW EACH
OTHER. THIS APPLIES TO ALL
COUNTS.

6 STEPS (8 THREADS WIDE)

START

FOR SQUARE END
START WITH 3.

4 STEPS (6 THREADS WIDE)

START

FOR SQUARE END,
START WITH 2, OVER
1 INTERSECTION, UP,
RIGHT, AND BACK TO
START.

3 STEPS (5 THREADS WIDE)

START ●———— NEEDLE COMES OUT ○———— NEEDLE GOES IN ————▶ DIRECTION OF ··········
NEEDLE ON BACK

MULTIPLE STEP HERRINGBONE*

This pattern is an extension of Double Herringbone (p. 46). Examples of 6 strands (over 8 threads), 4 strands (over 6 threads), and 3 strands (over 5 threads) are shown. Other large counts are possible. Double Herringbone is 2 strands (over 4 threads).

Try several shades of one color with an accent color for the last step.

* Left-handed people reverse "left" and "right."

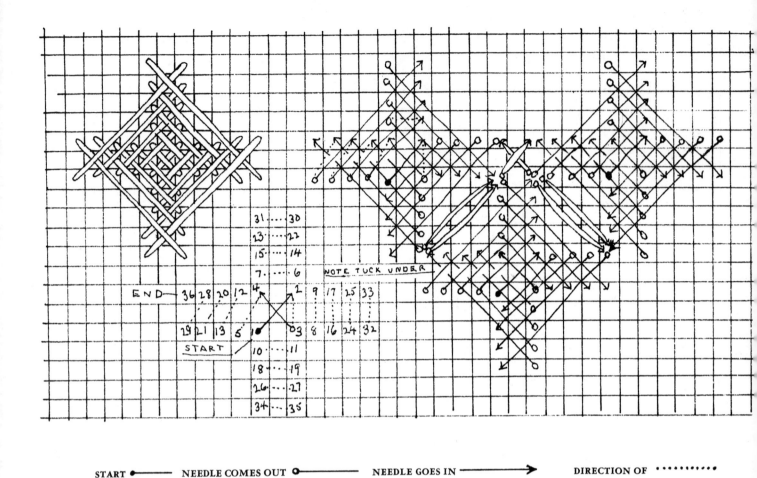

START ●——— NEEDLE COMES OUT ○———— NEEDLE GOES IN ————————➤ DIRECTION OF ··········
NEEDLE ON BACK

SQUARED HERRINGBONE

Use medium-fine yarn, 2 strands of Persian on No. 12 canvas.

Starting with a 2-thread cross stitch, 1, 2, 3, 4, follow the numbers on the diagram: odd numbers—needle comes out, even numbers—needle goes in.

In order to make the overlap of stitches uniform, pass the needle under stitch 5–6 before inserting it at 12. Do the same with stitch 19–20 under 13–14, 27–28 under 21–22, and 35–36 under 29–30.

Because of their shape, the units cannot be placed next to each other. Two diagonal stitches over 4 intersections at the sides and a diagonal cross at the ends of units will fill the spaces. Use heavy yarn in a contrasting color.

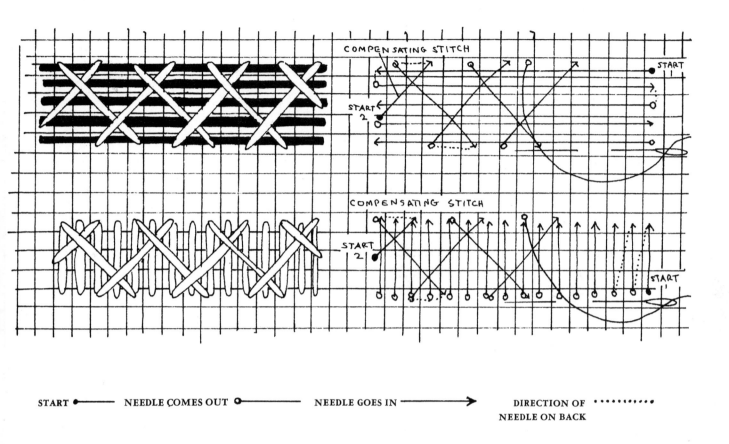

START ●━━━━ NEEDLE COMES OUT ○━━━━ NEEDLE GOES IN ━━━━▶ DIRECTION OF ••••••••••
NEEDLE ON BACK

HERRINGBONE COUCHING*

Regular Herringbone (p. 44) is worked over laid stitches. The diagrams show 5 horizontal laid strands and vertical stitches covering 4 threads. Many variations of these counts are possible. The Herringbone is usually worked in a contrasting color or material.

* Left-handed people reverse "left" and "right."

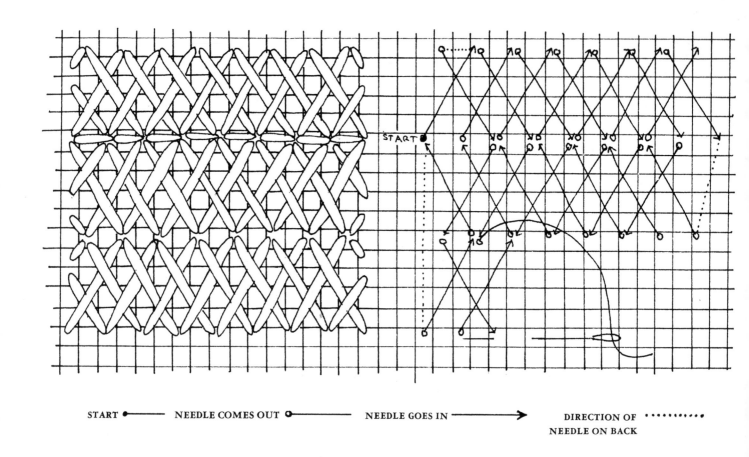

START ●━━━━ NEEDLE COMES OUT ○━━━━ NEEDLE GOES IN ━━━━▶ DIRECTION OF • • • • • • • • •
NEEDLE ON BACK

ALGERIAN PLAITED*

This is a tall Herringbone made like Closed Herringbone in surface stitchery. The yarn passes over 5 horizontal threads and 3 vertical threads. The needle goes under 2 vertical threads from right to left at top and bottom of row. Unless heavy yarn is used, back stitches over 2 threads will be needed between rows to cover canvas. Compensating stitches are shown at the ends of the rows in left diagram.

* Left-handed people reverse "left" and "right."

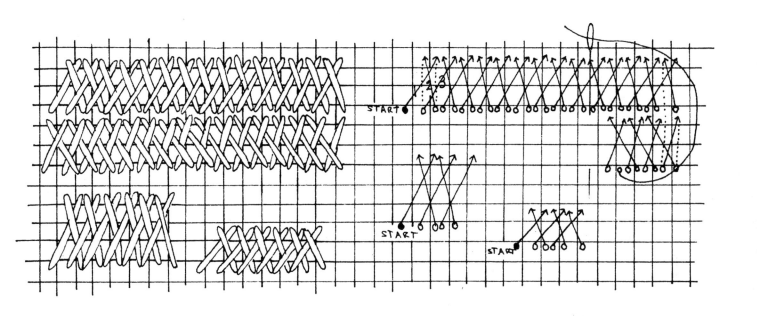

START ●————— NEEDLE COMES OUT ⦾————————— NEEDLE GOES IN —————————➤ DIRECTION OF ·········
NEEDLE ON BACK

PLAIT

The first stitch covers 2 vertical and 3 horizontal threads up, right. The second stitch covers 3 horizontal and *1* vertical threads up, left. The needle passes under 3 threads straight down for all stitches. Start the row at left. The progression of stitches is over 2 threads forward and 1 back, 2 forward and 1 back. Reverse the "lefts" and the "rights" in the second row.

The diagrams show this stitch pattern worked over 2, 3, and 4 horizontal threads.

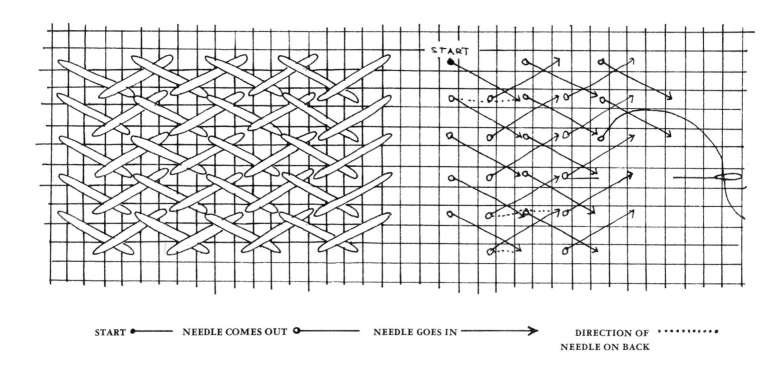

START ●———— NEEDLE COMES OUT O———— NEEDLE GOES IN ————➤ DIRECTION OF ••••••••••
                                                            NEEDLE ON BACK

PLAITED STITCH*

Work in vertical rows over 2 horizontal and 4 vertical threads, using every other hole. The stitches of the first row slant down to the right. The second row starts at the bottom, beginning 2 threads to the left of the end of the last stitch of row 1. These stitches slant up to the right over 4 vertical and 2 horizontal threads, and cross the stitches of row 1. The third row is like the first, the fourth like the second, etc. Heavy yarn is needed to cover the canvas.

* Left-handed people reverse "left" and "right."

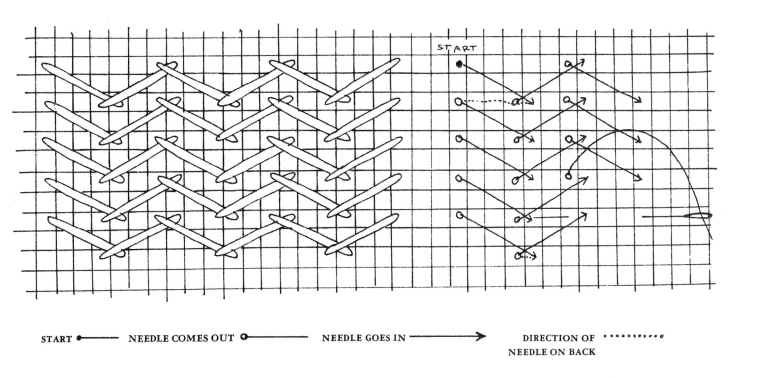

PLAITED GOBELIN*

This stitch pattern is similar to Plaited (p. 52) except that the stitches of the second row encroach over only 1 thread of first row instead of 2. Work in vertical rows over 4 vertical and 2 horizontal threads, using every other hole. The stitches slant down to the right in first row. The second row is worked from the bottom up, beginning 1 thread to the left of the end of the last stitch of row 1. These stitches slant up to the right over 4 vertical and 2 horizontal threads and cross the tips of the stitches of row 1. The third row starts 1 thread to the left of the end of the last stitch of row 2 and is made like row 1. The fourth row is like row 2, etc. Heavy yarn is needed to cover the canvas.

* Left-handed people reverse "left" and "right."

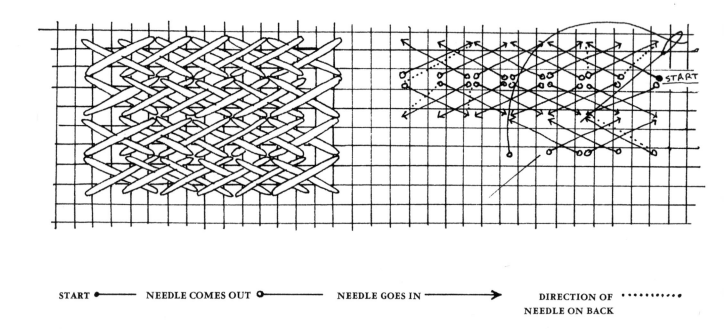

START •————— NEEDLE COMES OUT ⊙————— NEEDLE GOES IN ——————▶ DIRECTION OF •••••••••
NEEDLE ON BACK

KNITTING 1*

These are low flat overlapping cross stitches worked in horizontal rows. The first stitch covers 2 horizontal and 4 vertical threads up, left. Bring needle out 2 threads down. The second stitch covers 2 horizontal and 4 vertical threads up, right. Bring needle out 2 intersections down, left. Repeat these 2 stitches across row.

To work the second row with the same overlap of crosses as in first row, turn work halfway around (top at bottom) and work second row in this position, following directions as in row 1. Turn back around again for row 3.

* Left-handed people reverse "left" and "right."

54

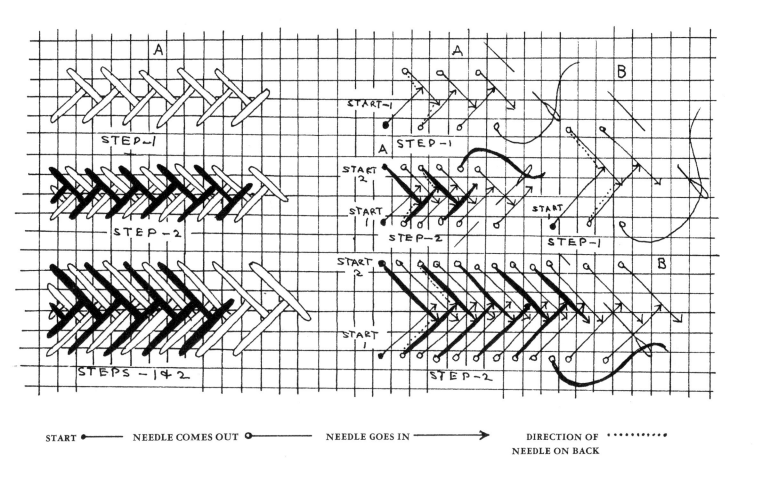

START ●——— NEEDLE COMES OUT ⊶——— NEEDLE GOES IN ——————▶ DIRECTION OF ••••••••••
NEEDLE ON BACK

DOUBLE FISHBONE

This pattern is related to Fishbone in surface stitchery. The rows are straight but the stitches are diagonal.

A. This version covers 3 threads.

Step 1. Begin with a stitch covering 2 intersections, up, right. Pass the needle under 1 intersection, up, left. Make a stitch over 2 intersections, down, right. Pass the needle under 1 intersection, down, left. Make another stitch over 2 intersections, up, right, like stitch 1. Repeat stitch 2, and continue in this manner. You will use every other hole along the top and bottom of the row.

Step 2. With a contrasting color, start 3 threads directly above start of step 1. Using the vacant holes, make stitches as in step 1. These stitches will partially cover the stitches of step 1.

B. This is a wider version covering 5 threads. The stitches cover 3 intersections, and the needle passes under 2 intersections. Note compensating stitches to form straight ends in diagram at left.

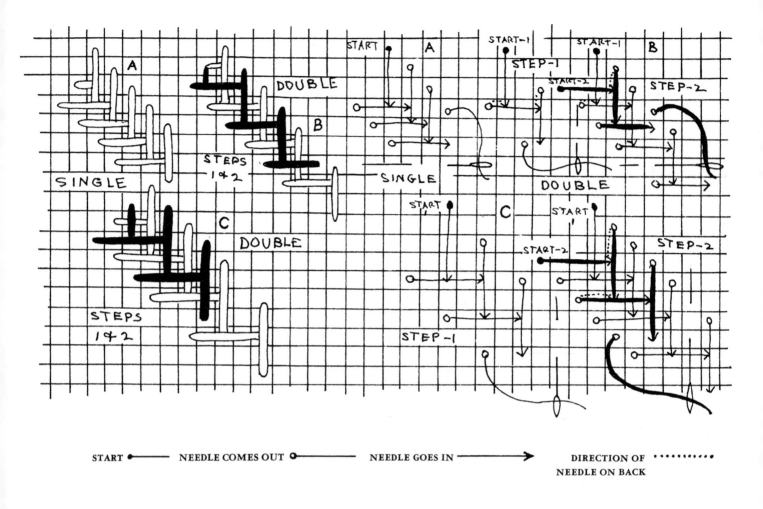

START ●————— NEEDLE COMES OUT ○————— NEEDLE GOES IN ————▶ DIRECTION OF •••••••••
NEEDLE ON BACK

DIAGONAL DOUBLE FISHBONE

In this version, the rows are diagonal, but the stitches are straight. Heavier yarn will be needed than in the straight row version to cover the canvas.

A. Single. This is not strictly Double Fishbone, but it is produced in a similar manner. Start with a vertical stitch down over 3 threads. Pass the needle under 2 threads to the left, and make a horizontal stitch over 3 threads to the right, covering the tip of stitch 1. Pass the needle up under 2 threads, and make another vertical stitch down over 3 threads. Pass the needle under 2 threads, and continue.

B. Double. Step 1. Start with a vertical stitch over 3 threads. This time pass the needle under only 1 thread to the left. Make a horizontal stitch over 3 threads, and pass the needle up under 1 thread. Continue these vertical and horizontal stitches. Step 1 uses every other hole in a diagonal line down, right.

Step 2. Start 2 intersections down, left from start of step 1. Make a horizontal stitch over 3 threads, and over first stitch of step 1. Pass the needle up under 1 thread. Make a vertical stitch over 3 threads and stitch 2 of step 1. Continue as in step 1, using intervening holes between stitches of step 1.

C. This is a wider version. The stitches cover 4 threads, and the needle passes under 2 threads.
Note compensating stitches in left diagrams for straight ends.
By reversing "left" and "right" the row will slant diagonally down, left.

56

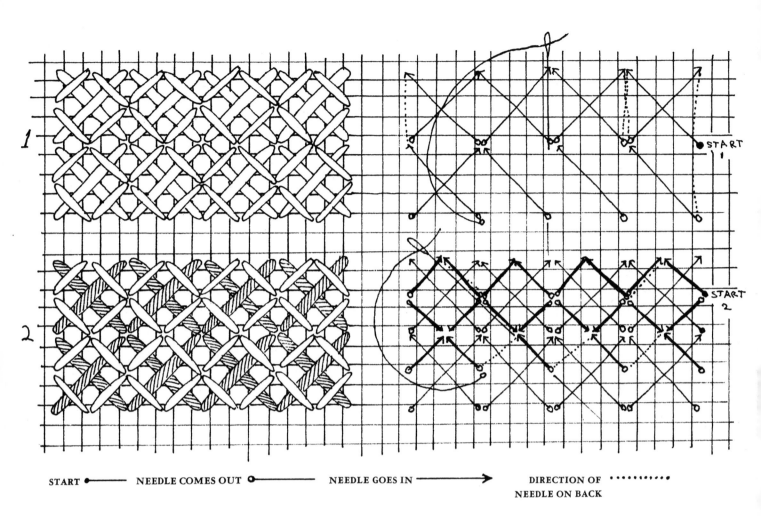

START ●———— NEEDLE COMES OUT ○———— NEEDLE GOES IN ————→ DIRECTION OF ••••••••••
NEEDLE ON BACK

RICE
Crossed Corners

There are two steps to this pattern. They can both be worked in the same color (1) or step 2 can be worked in a contrasting color (2). The left diagrams show the two steps for both forms. Use heavier yarn for step 1 than for step 2 to cover the canvas well.

Step 1. Work first stitches of large diagonal crosses in journey from right to left over 4 intersections from lower right to upper left. The needle goes under 4 threads straight down. Go all the way across row. Use the *same* holes for the return journey with stitches going from lower left to upper right to complete the crosses.

Step 2. If desired the 4 stitches that go over the arms of the large cross can be worked a unit at a time, forming a diamond or diagonal square. It is simpler and produces a more uniform stitch to work a stitch over upper right arm of each cross from right to left. Then on return journey, make the stitches over upper left arm. Repeat for 2 lower arms.

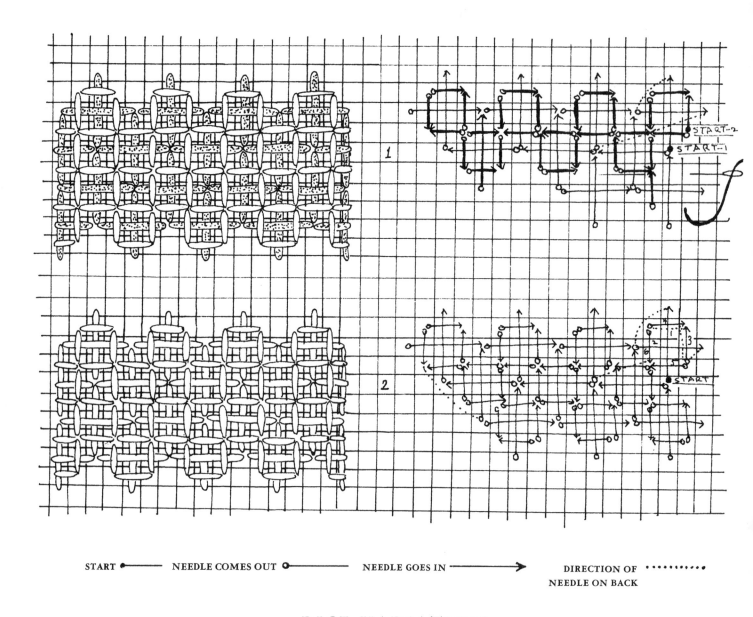

RICE VARIATION

This stitch pattern could be called Straight Rice.

1. Start with large straight crosses over 4 threads each way, fitting the second row up between crosses of first row. Then work vertical and horizontal stitches over the arms of the crosses and 2 threads in a contrasting color.

2. Version 2 is worked all in one color. Complete each unit before starting the next. Follow the numbers in the diagram. Diagram at left shows compensation at the sides for straight vertical edges. For geometric designs, this pattern fits against a diagonal line without compensation.

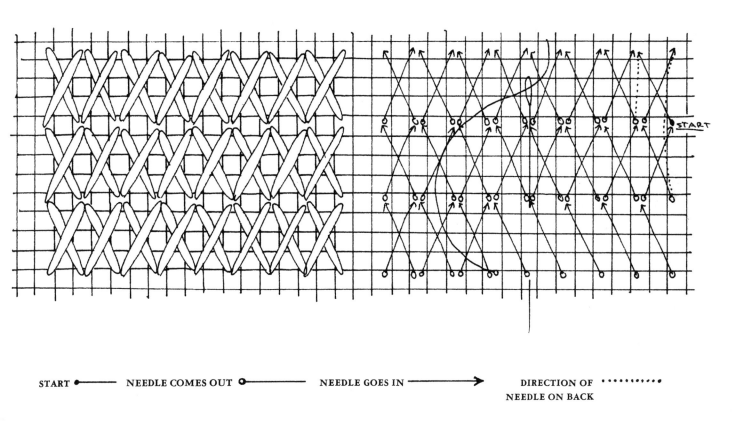

START ●———— NEEDLE COMES OUT ○————— NEEDLE GOES IN ————▶ DIRECTION OF ••••••••••
NEEDLE ON BACK

OBLONG CROSS

This stitch pattern is worked the same as Diagonal Cross (p. 25) except that the crosses cover 4 horizontal and 2 vertical threads. Starting at the right, work a row of slanting stitches covering 2 vertical and 4 horizontal threads, using every other hole. Complete the crosses on return journey, using the same holes.

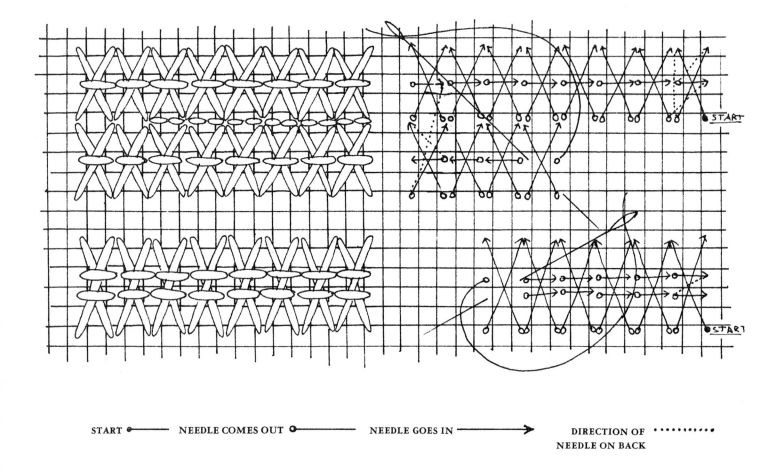

OBLONG CROSS WITH BACK STITCH

Work a complete oblong cross over 2 vertical and 4 horizontal threads, bringing the needle out 2 threads down on left side of cross. Insert needle 2 threads down on right side and bring it out in same hole as lower left leg of cross stitch. Repeat across row. In the second row the order of the stitches is reversed, the back stitches starting on the right side of cross.

In the second version of this pattern the crosses covering 5 horizontal threads and 2 back stitches are placed across the middle, one below the other.

If canvas threads show between rows, they may be covered with small back stitches, 1 to a thread.

60

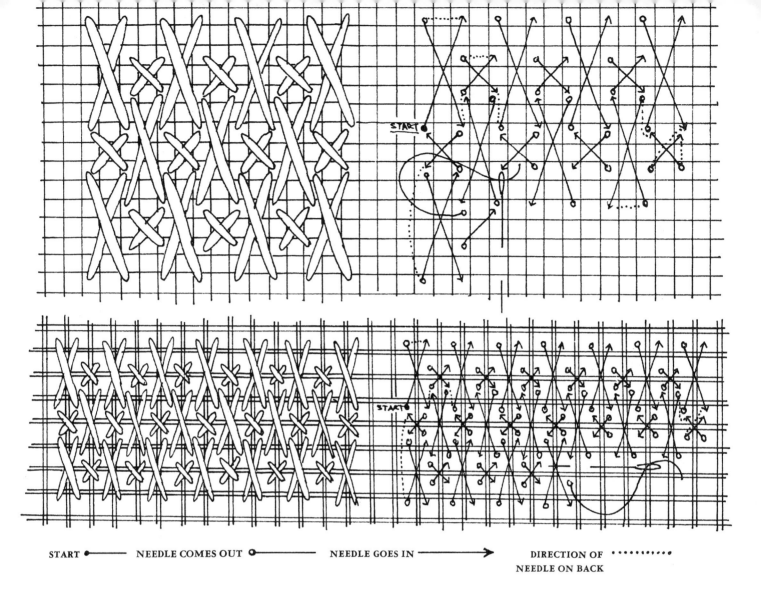

START ●————— NEEDLE COMES OUT ○————— NEEDLE GOES IN ————————▶ DIRECTION OF ••••••••••
NEEDLE ON BACK

LARGE OBLONG CROSS 1
Double Stitch

Starting at left, work a large oblong cross over 6 horizontal and 2 vertical threads. Then, 2 threads down, opposite the middle of the oblong cross, make a diagonal cross over 2 intersections each way. Continue these 2 stitches across the row. In the second row the large crosses fit up under diagonal crosses of first row and vice versa. Turn halfway around to work second and fourth rows.

An interesting effect can be obtained by using contrasting colors for the two types of crosses. Heavy yarn must be used to cover canvas.

The small size of this stitch pattern must be made on double mesh canvas as the needle would have to be passed under only 1 thread, which is not recommended for single mesh canvas. The stitches would not stay in place.

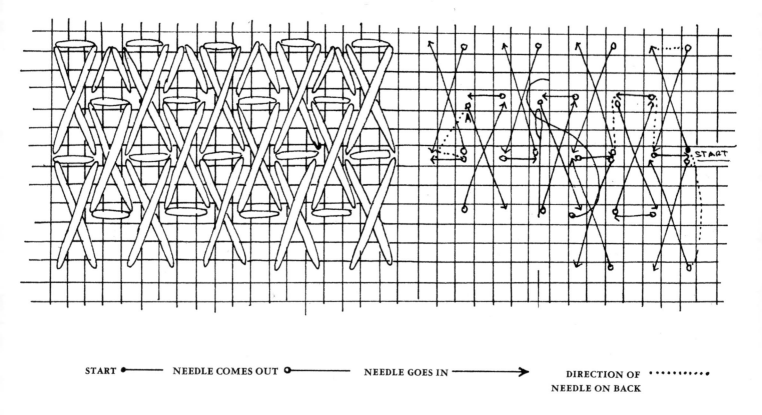

START ●————— NEEDLE COMES OUT ○————— NEEDLE GOES IN ————————▶ DIRECTION OF ●●●●●●●●●●●
NEEDLE ON BACK

LARGE OBLONG CROSS 2

Work large oblong cross stitch over 6 horizontal and 2 vertical threads. Then, 3 threads down, opposite the middle of the cross, make a horizontal stitch over 2 threads. Continue across row. In the second row make horizontal stitch across bottom of legs of crosses of first row and fit crosses up between them. In order to have the same overlap of crosses in second row as in first, start crosses at top (A).

The diagram at left shows compensating stitches at top. Use heavy yarn to cover canvas.

62

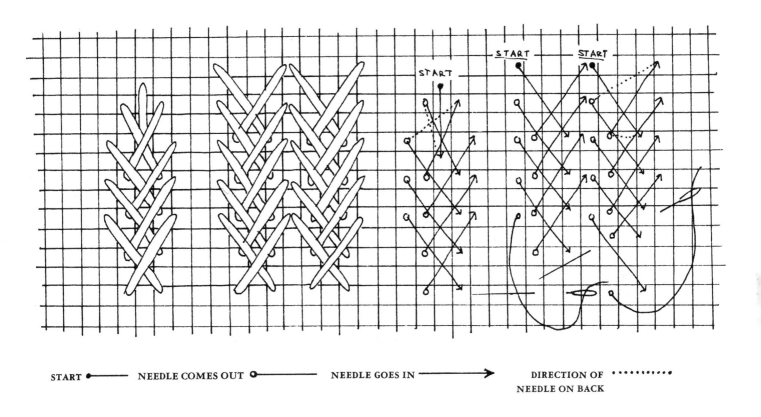

START ●——— NEEDLE COMES OUT ○——— NEEDLE GOES IN ———→ DIRECTION OF ●●●●●●●●●●
NEEDLE ON BACK

FERN*

Work in vertical rows using every other hole. Start at top, left. Insert needle 4 threads down and 3 threads to right. Bring needle out 2 threads to left, and insert it 4 threads to right of your starting point. Bring needle out 2 threads below starting point and repeat. Heavy yarn is required. Start all rows at the top.

Tapered tip. Starting at the top, make a vertical stitch over 4 threads. Bring needle out 1 intersection down, left, from starting point. Make the second stitch over 4 horizontal and 2 vertical threads down, right. Bring the needle out 2 threads to the left and make a matching stitch over the same vertical and horizontal threads up, right. Bring needle out 2 horizontal and 1 vertical threads down, left, from beginning of second stitch and proceed with regular Fern stitch.

* Left-handed people reverse "left" and "right."

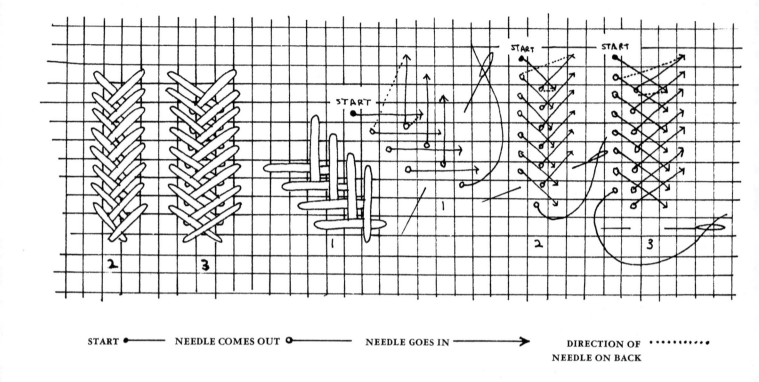

START ●——— NEEDLE COMES OUT O——————— NEEDLE GOES IN ————————▶ DIRECTION OF •••••••••
NEEDLE ON BACK

FERN VARIATIONS*

1. Diagonal. The first stitch is over 4 vertical threads, left to right. Bring needle out 1 intersection down, left. Make the second stitch over 4 horizontal threads, up, and bring needle out 1 intersection down, right, from beginning of first stitch. Repeat. The row of stitches proceeds diagonally down, right.

2. The first stitch covers 2 intersections down, right. Bring needle out 1 thread to the left. The second stitch covers 2 intersections up, right. Bring needle out 1 hole below beginning of first stitch. The pattern covers a row 3 threads wide. Leave yarn fairly loose or center stitch under 1 thread will slip out of place.

3. The first stitch covers 3 vertical and 2 horizontal threads down, right. Bring the needle out 2 threads to the left. The second stitch covers 3 vertical and 2 horizontal threads up, right. Bring needle out 1 hole below beginning of first stitch. The pattern covers a row 4 threads wide. Start all rows at the top. Heavy yarn is required.

* Left-handed people reverse "left" and "right."

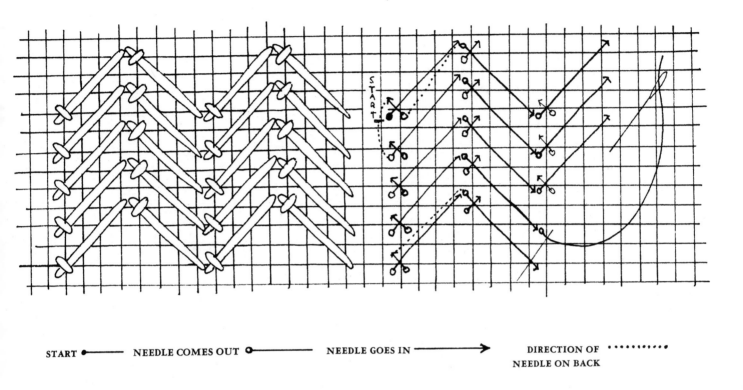

START ●——— NEEDLE COMES OUT o——— NEEDLE GOES IN ———→ DIRECTION OF ••••••••••
NEEDLE ON BACK

FISHBONE*

Begin first stitch 4 threads down on left side of area to be covered. Make a stitch over 4 intersections up, right, and place a Tent stitch across the starting end of the stitch. Bring needle out 2 threads below beginning of first stitch and repeat. Work in vertical rows, alternating direction of stitches to form a zigzag. Heavy yarn is needed to cover canvas.

* Left-handed people reverse "left" and "right."

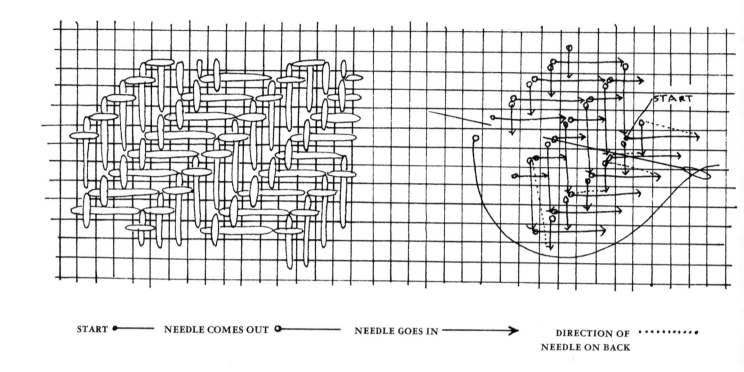

START •————— NEEDLE COMES OUT O————— NEEDLE GOES IN ————————▶ DIRECTION OF • • • • • • • • • •
NEEDLE ON BACK

DIAGONAL FISHBONE

The stitches are vertical and horizontal, but the rows are diagonal. The stitches cover 4 threads, the rows alternating vertical and horizontal. A short stitch covering 2 threads crosses the long stitch 1 thread in from its beginning.

Diagram at left shows some compensation for straight edges. Because compensation is rather difficult, make first row across wide part of area to be covered. Work to the bottom, compensating along the sides as you go. Now turn your work halfway around (top at bottom). Fitting a row up to your first row, work to the bottom again.

66

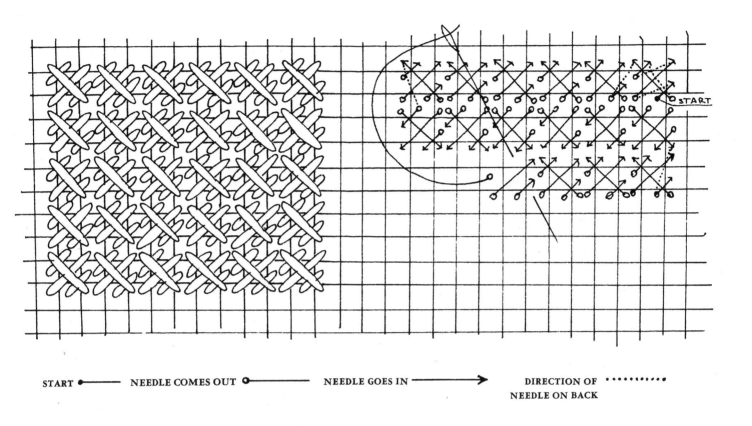

START ●━━━━ NEEDLE COMES OUT ○━━━━ NEEDLE GOES IN ━━━▶ DIRECTION OF ••••••••••
NEEDLE ON BACK

CROSSED MOSAIC*

This stitch pattern is best worked in horizontal rows.

Row 1.   Make the 3 stitches as in regular Mosaic (p. 98), beginning at lower right. Bring needle out 1 thread to right of beginning of first stitch, and insert it at top left, 1 thread to left of end of third stitch so a diagonal stitch crosses the little square. Repeat across row.

Row 2.   Turn the work halfway around (top at bottom) and follow directions for row 1.

* Left-handed people turn diagram halfway around (top at the bottom) and start in lower left corner.

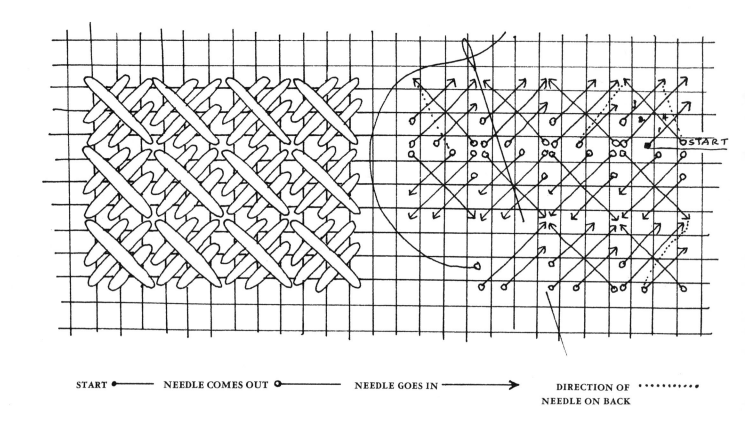

CROSSED SCOTCH*

Make 3 diagonal stitches, crossing 2, 3, 2 intersections. Bring needle out 2 threads to right of starting point and make a crossing stitch over 3 intersections and the 3 stitches. Turn the work halfway around (top at bottom) and follow directions for row 1.

* Left-handed people turn diagram halfway around (top at bottom) and start in lower left corner.

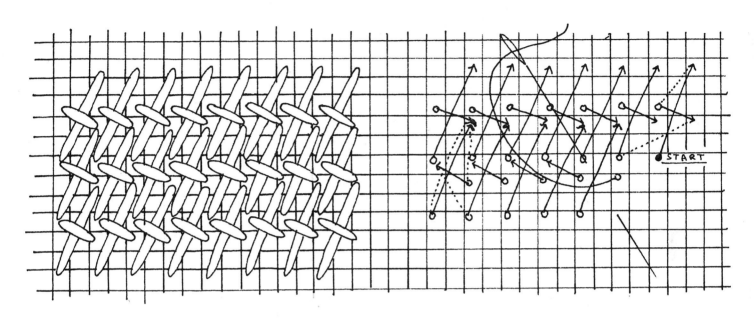

KNOTTED

Make a slanting stitch over 2 vertical and 5 horizontal threads, up, right. Bring needle out 2 intersections down, left. Make a shorter stitch over long stitch and 1 horizontal and 2 vertical threads, down, right. Bring needle out 2 threads to left of start of first stitch and repeat across row. The second row starts 3 threads down from beginning of last long stitch and fits up between stitches of first row, the top of the long stitch using the same hole as right end of short stitch of first row. To make the short stitch in the opposite direction bring the needle out 3 threads below top end of long stitch.

69

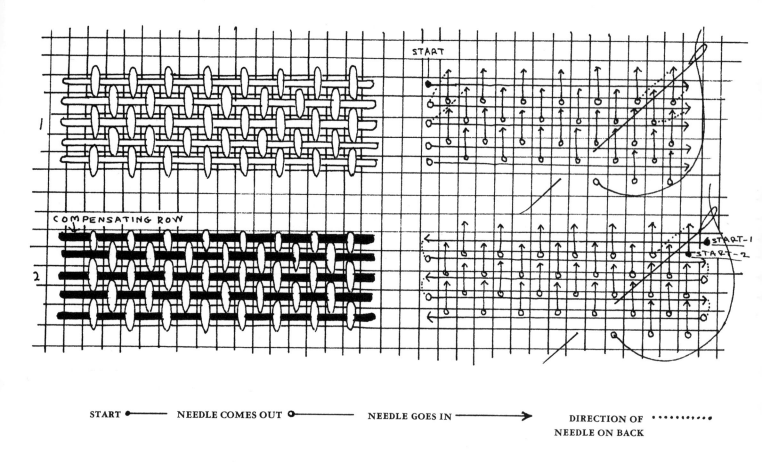

START ●——— NEEDLE COMES OUT ⦶——— NEEDLE GOES IN ———▶ DIRECTION OF ••••••••••
NEEDLE ON BACK

BOKHARA COUCHING 1 & 2*

1. There are many variations possible for this stitch pattern. These, and variations 3 and 4, have proved useful for background. The effect created is that of a woven material. Version 1 is produced with 1 strand of yarn. Bring the needle out at left end of row and lay a strand of yarn between 2 horizontal threads. Bring the needle out 1 intersection down, left, and make vertical stitches over laid strand and 2 horizontal threads, using every other hole. The needle passes under 2 intersections. To begin second row bring needle out 1 thread below beginning of laid strand of first row. Lay a strand as in first row between next pair of horizontal threads. This time bring the needle out either straight down under 1 thread or 1 thread down and 2 threads to the left. Make vertical threads as in first row, using the spaces between stitches of first row. Stitches encroach over 1 thread of first row. All stitches on the back are in one direction, causing some distortion.

2. In this version 2 strands are used, 1 for the laid strand and 1 for the covering stitches. This enables you to use different thicknesses of yarn or different colors. Strictly speaking this is not Bokhara Couching because 2 strands are used, but the effect and method are very similar. The rows alternate in direction. The back of this stitch pattern looks like Diagonal Weaving. Because the stitches on the back alternate in direction, there is no distortion in this version.

It is best not to try to piece laid strand. It can be done, but it is best to carry it all the way across. The laid strand and covering stitch strand can be passed under other work for short distances.

In the compensating row at top of the lower left diagram, the vertical stitches cover the laid strand and only one canvas thread.

* Left-handed people reverse "left" and "right."

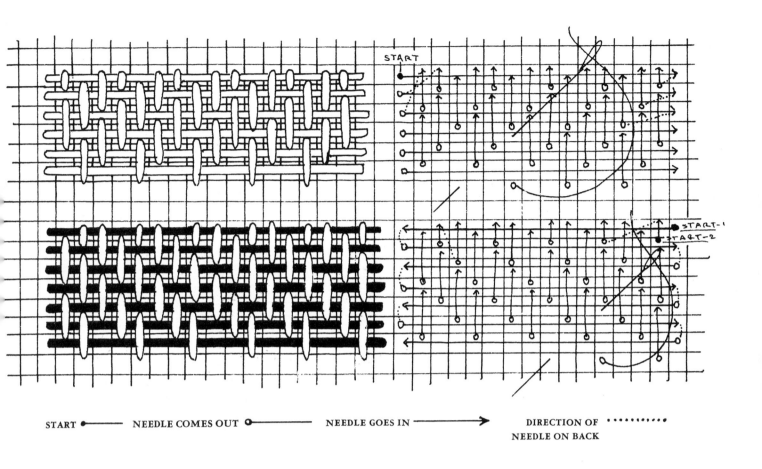

START •——— NEEDLE COMES OUT ⚬——— NEEDLE GOES IN ——→ DIRECTION OF ••••••••• NEEDLE ON BACK

BOKHARA COUCHING 3 & 4*

3. This is worked with 1 strand as in Bokhara Couching 1. Lay a strand from left to right. Cover it and *1* horizontal thread, the lower one, using every *third* hole. In the second row lay the strand and make the vertical stitches over 2 horizontal threads and *both* laid strands, again using every third hole, with stitches beside those of first row, either side. These first two rows are compensating rows. In the third and subsequent rows the stitches cover *2* laid strands and *3* horizontal threads, encroaching over 1 thread of previous row. The pattern of stitches progresses diagonally down either left or right. Because all stitches on the back are in one direction, this version can distort the canvas.

4. Use separate strands for this version as in Bokhara Couching 2. The first two rows show compensation. The rows alternate in direction. Different weights and colors of yarn can be used. Strictly speaking this is not Bokhara Couching because 2 strands of yarn are used, but the method and effect are very similar. Because the stitches on the back alternate in direction, there is no distortion in this version.

* Left-handed people reverse "left" and "right."

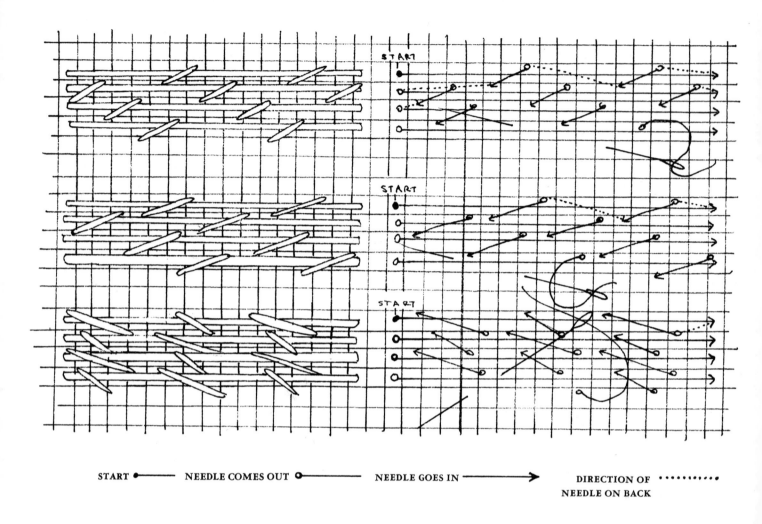

START •——— NEEDLE COMES OUT ⊶——— NEEDLE GOES IN ———→ DIRECTION OF •••••••••
                                                                         NEEDLE ON BACK

ROUMANIAN COUCHING 1*

    Long strands are laid from left to right, using every hole. On the return journey make slanting stitches at intervals over laid strand, 1 horizontal thread, and varying numbers of vertical threads. Many arrangements are possible. The slanting stitches are supposed to be relatively inconspicuous. Don't piece laid strand if you can help it.

---

* Left-handed people reverse "left" and "right."

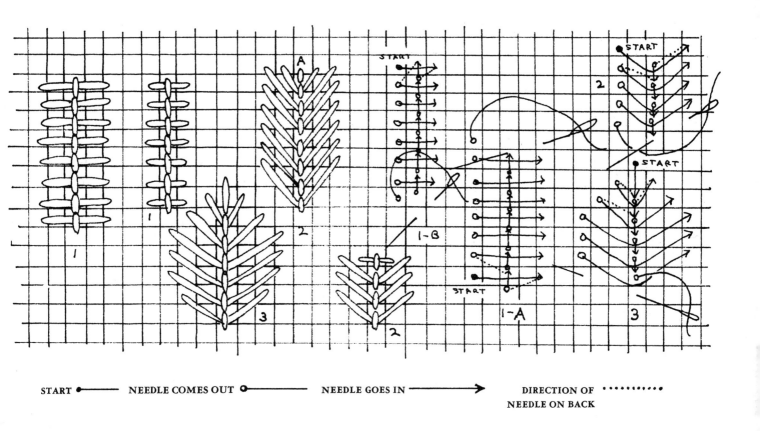

START ●————— NEEDLE COMES OUT ○————— NEEDLE GOES IN ————→ DIRECTION OF •••••••••••
                                                          NEEDLE ON BACK

ROUMANIAN COUCHING 2*
Fly Stitch

This stitch pattern is worked in vertical rows. Start at either top or bottom.

1. Bring needle out at left side of area and make first stitch over an even number of threads (2, 4, 6) to the right. Have working strand up. Bring needle out in center hole, 1 thread below level of first stitch. Insert needle up over 1 thread and first stitch, and bring it out 1 hole above (or below) start of first stitch. Repeat. You can start a row at either the bottom or top (1-A and 1-B).

2. Start this form at top of row at left side of area. Insert needle at right over an even number of threads (4, 6, 8). Have working strand down. Bring needle out in middle hole 1 or 2 threads below ends of first stitch, depending on depth of angle desired. Insert needle down over 1 thread and first stitch, forming it into a V. Bring needle out 1 hole below start of first stitch and repeat. If a straight edge at top of row is desired, a horizontal stitch over 2 threads and a vertical stitch over 1 thread (for shallow V), or a vertical stitch over the middle thread, then a smaller V-shaped group over 2 threads (A) can be made before starting directions for no. 2.

3. *Leaf shape.* Start this version at top with a vertical stitch over 2 threads. Bring needle out 1 hole diagonally down, left from start of first stitch. Insert needle at right of first stitch 1 hole diagonally down, right, and, with working strand down, bring needle out at base of first stitch. Make a stitch down over 1 thread and second stitch, forming it into a deep V. Bring needle out 1 hole diagonally down, left, from start of second stitch. Insert needle 1 hole down, right, from end of second stitch, and bring it out at base of first short stitch. Make a stitch down over 1 thread and long stitch. Make 3 or more groups with long stitches covering 6 threads, depending on length of leaf desired. Last, make a group with long stitch covering 4 threads. By varying the length of long stitches, different shaped leaves can be obtained. Versions of this stitch pattern whose long stitches are straight will require heavier yarn than those whose long stitches slant.

* Left-handed people reverse "left" and "right."

73

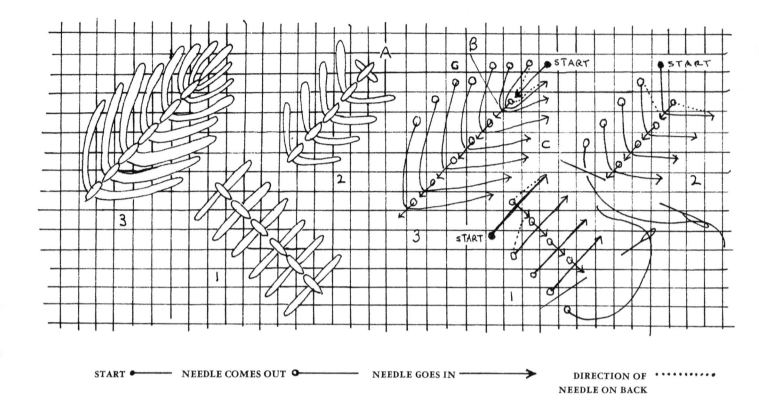

START ●———— NEEDLE COMES OUT ○———————— NEEDLE GOES IN ————————▶ DIRECTION OF ●●●●●●●●●●●
NEEDLE ON BACK

DIAGONAL ROUMANIAN COUCHING

1. Start at upper left of row. Make a stitch up, right, over 3 intersections. Bring needle out 2 threads to left and 1 thread down. Make a short stitch over first stitch and 1 intersection down, right. Bring needle out 1 hole down, right, from start of first stitch and repeat. By reversing "left" and "right" the row will slant down, left.

2. Make a stitch over 3 intersections down, right, and, with working strand to left, bring needle out 2 threads down and 1 thread to right of start of first stitch, forming it into an L or a diagonal V. Insert needle down, left, over 1 intersection and first stitch. Bring needle out 1 hole down, left, from start of first stitch and repeat. To make a straight edge at beginning of row make a diagonal cross stitch over 1 intersection with top stitch running from upper right to lower left (A) before starting directions for stitch 2. By reversing "left" and "right" the row will slant down, right.

3. *Leaf shape.* Make a diagonal stitch over 2 intersections down, left. Bring needle out 1 thread to left of start of first stitch. Insert needle 1 thread below start of first stitch and, with working strand to left, bring needle out at end of first stitch, forming second stitch into a deep V. Insert needle over second stitch and 1 intersection down, left, bringing it out 1 thread to left of start of second stitch. In order to reduce the angle of subsequent stitches, pass needle under the short stitch of first group (B). Insert needle 1 thread below end of stitch 2. Make the next 2 groups even at the ends (C). Make two or more groups with long stitches starting and ending 1 intersection down, left. By varying length of long stitches, different shaped leaves can be obtained.

Heavy yarn is needed to cover canvas.

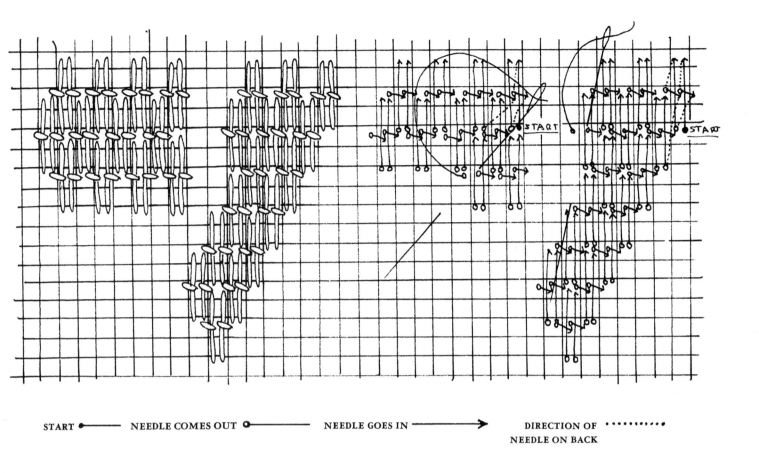

START ●————— NEEDLE COMES OUT ○————— NEEDLE GOES IN ————→ DIRECTION OF • • • • • • • • • •
NEEDLE ON BACK

FRENCH 1

There are two versions of row sequence. Stitch units can form rows that progress down to the left or they can be worked in horizontal rows, using every other hole. The results of either method are the same.

Be sure to use fine yarn for French 1 as 2 stitches are made in each hole. Work a vertical stitch over 4 threads and bring needle out 2 threads straight down and thread to the left of first stitch. Make a small horizontal stitch over first stitch and 1 vertical thread to the right, bringing needle out in same hole as beginning of first stitch. Insert needle in same hole at the top and bring needle out 2 threads down and 1 thread to the left. Insert needle between vertical stitches. For slanting row bring needle out 4 threads down (2 below bottom of first unit) and 1 thread to the left. Repeat unit of 4 stitches. For horizontal row bring needle out 2 threads to the left of bottoms of vertical stitches of first unit. The units of second row fit up between those of first row.

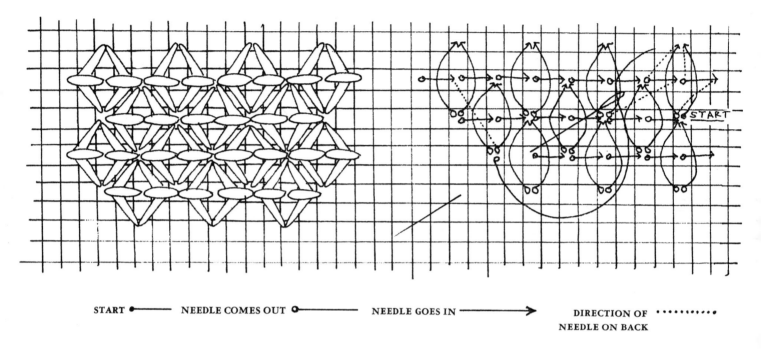

FRENCH 2*

Make a vertical stitch over 4 threads. Before pulling the stitch tight, bring the needle out 2 threads below the top of stitch. Insert needle 2 threads to the right, and bring it out in the same hole as the start of the first stitch. Insert needle at top in same hole as stitch 1, and bring it out 2 intersections down, left. Insert needle at left end of the horizontal stitch and bring it out 4 threads to the left of base of first and third stitches. Repeat these 4 stitches.

The horizontal stitches will be touching, end to end. The units of second row fit up between units of first row, starting 2 threads down, and 2 threads right or left. This pattern will fit well against a diagonal line.

* Left-handed people reverse "left" and "right."

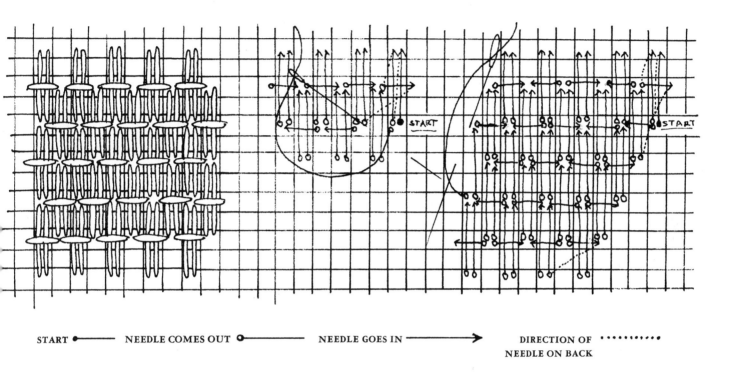

START ●━━━━ NEEDLE COMES OUT ⊶━━━━ NEEDLE GOES IN ━━━▶ DIRECTION OF •••••••••
NEEDLE ON BACK

DOUBLE TIE*
Paris

Make 2 vertical stitches over 4 threads in 1 hole, the right one first. Bring needle out 2 threads down and 1 thread to the left.

Make a horizontal stitch over the 2 stitches and 2 threads. Bring needle out 4 threads down from start of tie stitch and repeat. Rows slant down to the left, and then up to the right.

This stitch pattern is similar to French 1 (p. 75) except 1 horizontal stitch covers both vertical stitches instead of 1 each. It can be worked in horizontal rows.

* Left-handed people reverse "left" and "right."

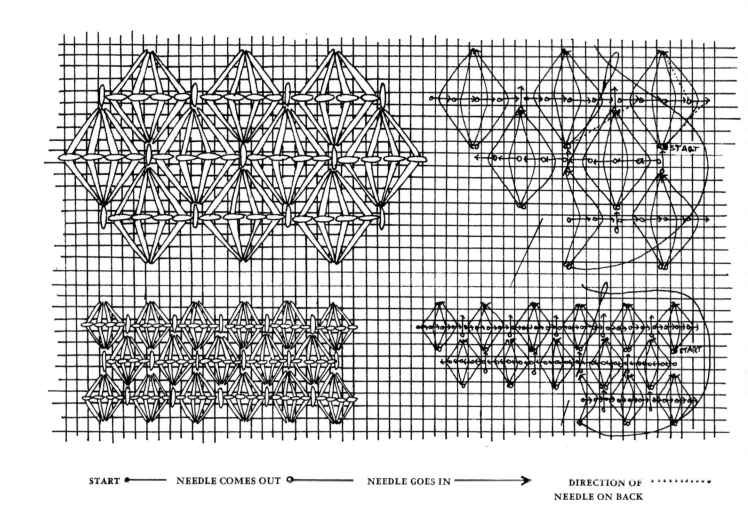

START ●——— NEEDLE COMES OUT ○——————— NEEDLE GOES IN ————————▶ DIRECTION OF ···········•
NEEDLE ON BACK

ROCOCO 1 & 2

The long stitches of this stitch pattern are worked over 8 horizontal threads and are caught down with short stitches beginning 4 threads down and 3 threads to the right. The short stitches cover 2 vertical threads. The second unit starts 8 threads to the left of beginning of first unit. The second row fits up between units of first row, starting 5 threads down. A vertical stitch covering 2 threads is placed between units to cover exposed threads.

The smaller version is worked the same way except that the vertical stitches cover 4 threads and the short tie stitches are made over only 1 thread.

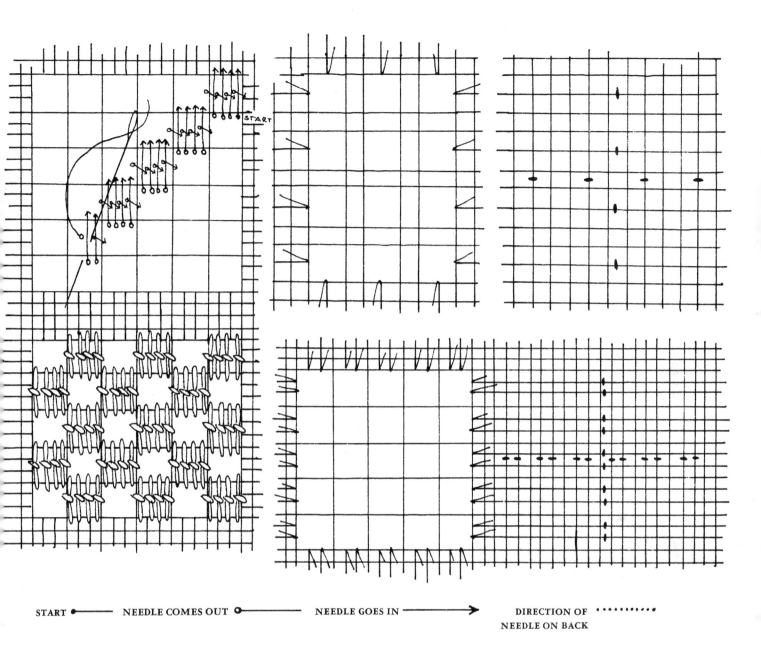

START ●———— NEEDLE COMES OUT O———— NEEDLE GOES IN ————————▶ DIRECTION OF ●●●●●●●●●●●
NEEDLE ON BACK

ROCOCO 3

Because there are 4 stitch units in a group, you must either use very large canvas, 5 holes to the inch, or remove some of the canvas threads on the portion of the work to be covered by this stitch pattern. For small areas these can be cut, raveled back, and fastened to the back of the remaining canvas, to be held in place by other stitch patterns. For large areas remove the threads a little at a time as required so that the canvas will be easier to handle. The obvious plan of removing every other thread must be avoided because to do so destroys the over-under weave of the canvas, and there would be no way to keep the remaining threads in place. So for medium size canvas remove 1 thread and leave 2. These will not be evenly spaced but the stitching will make them even. On fine canvas remove 2 threads and leave 1 to produce holes large enough to accommodate the stitch pattern.

Each unit consists of 4 vertical stitches caught down by short slanting stitches, the first and fourth of which also cover the adjacent vertical threads. Rows progress down, left. This stitch pattern is similar to French 1 (p. 75).

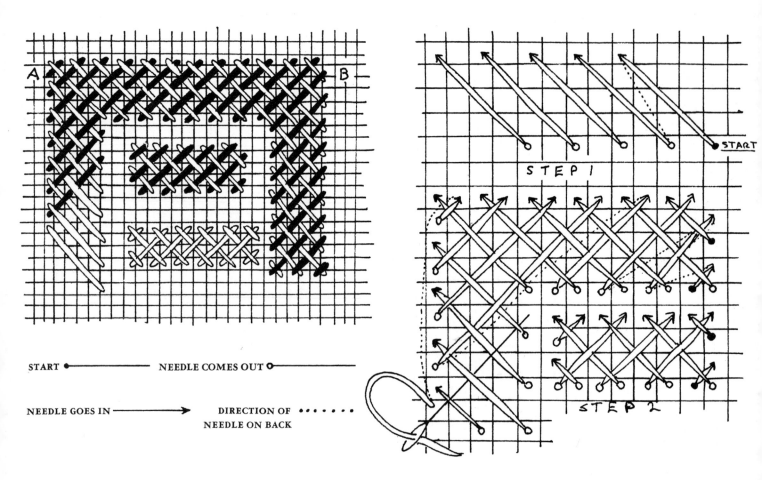

START •————— NEEDLE COMES OUT ○————————

NEEDLE GOES IN ——————→   DIRECTION OF • • • • • •
                                     NEEDLE ON BACK

WOVEN BAND

Step 1. Work diagonal stitches over 3, 4, or 5 intersections in a horizontal row, using every other hole, from right to left.

Step 2. Beginning at either end and using the holes between ends of stitches in step 1, work diagonal stitches pointing in the opposite direction. Between stitches weave needle under and over stitches of step 1 to form a lattice work or weaving.

This stitch is effective when contrasting colors are used. It is possible to work corners. An uneven number of threads between corners produces sharp angle corners (A). If you have an even number of threads, a slightly rounded corner can be made at one end (B).

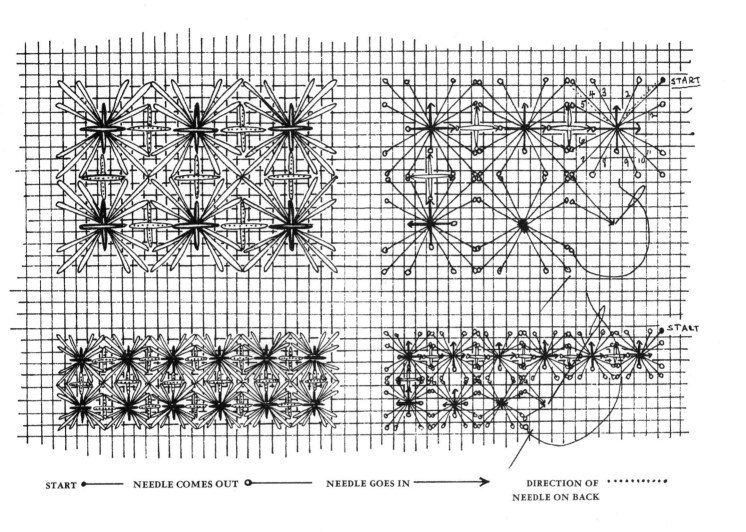

LEVIATHAN

Start with a diagonal stitch in upper right corner over 4 intersections (1). Bring needle out 2 holes to left of starting point and insert it in same hole as first stitch (2). Skip 4 threads and reverse first 2 stitches, using same hole in center (3 and 4), and add a third stitch beginning 2 threads down from start of stitch no. 4 (5). Continue around square with these groups of 3 stitches, ending with the third stitch of first group (12). Then make a Straight Cross over 4 threads in the middle. Repeat these groups over area. Fill open spaces between and below squares with a 4 thread Straight Cross in a contrasting color. Heavy yarn must be used to cover canvas.

The smaller version of this stitch pattern uses finer yarn. It is really a variation of Algerian Eye (p. 123) combined with Straight Cross (p. 31).

A third contrasting color can be used over the center of the square.

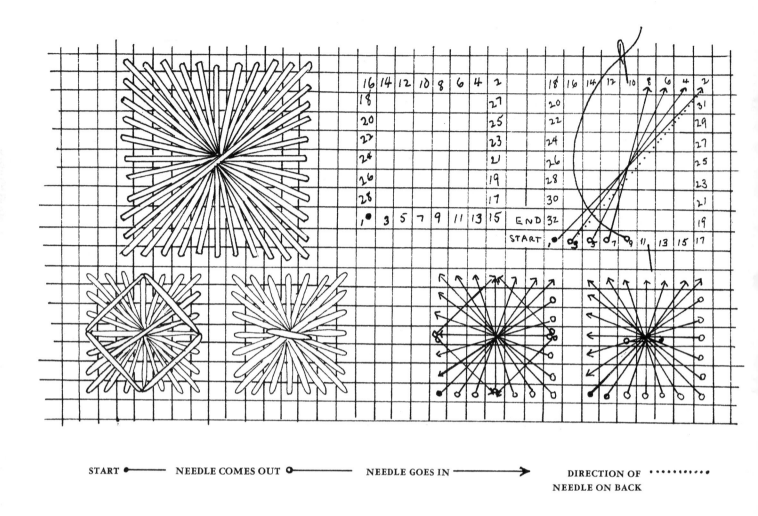

START ●——— NEEDLE COMES OUT ○——— NEEDLE GOES IN ———→ DIRECTION OF ··········· NEEDLE ON BACK

RHODES

These squares can be made to any count. The accumulation of layers of yarn in the center causes it to be very high. From the side, the unit somewhat resembles a pyramid. An uneven number of holes, even number of threads, along a side must be used if the extra stitches, as in the lower diagrams, are to be added.

Make the first stitch diagonally across the desired number of intersections (1–2). Then by moving the starts of each stitch to the right, and the ends to the left, continue on around the square. Follow the numbers in the diagram at top, right. The needle passes across under the unit. The extra stitches are added last.

82

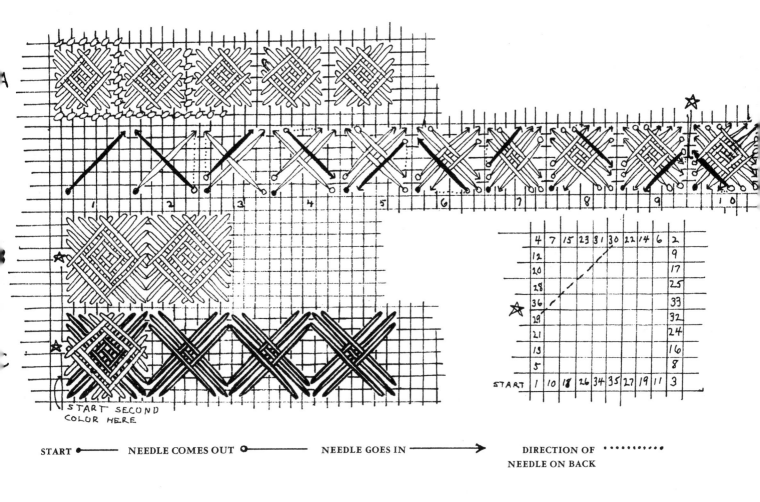

WAFFLE
Norwich

A   Five-Thread Square.   Make a large diagonal cross over 5 threads each way (1 and 2). Passing the needle under the threads along the outside edge, work around the square, clockwise. Follow the steps for diagram A through 9. Before finishing stitch 10, pass the needle under stitch 7 (see star in diagram 10). This pattern is effective when 1 thread is left between squares to be covered with Continental Tent (p. 89) in a darker color.

B   Seven-Thread Square.   This is worked in the same manner as the 5-thread square, but there are 14 stitches to each unit. It is particularly handsome when a darker value is used for the first 6 stitches, and a lighter value of the same color is used for the top 8 stitches. Be sure to pass the needle under stitch 11 before finishing the last stitch (see star).

C   For larger squares, any uneven number of threads can be used. For a 9-thread square follow numbers in diagram at right; out at uneven numbers, in at even. Be sure to pass last stitch (35–36) under (29–30) before putting needle in at 36 (☆). For larger sizes eliminate Continental Tent stitches.

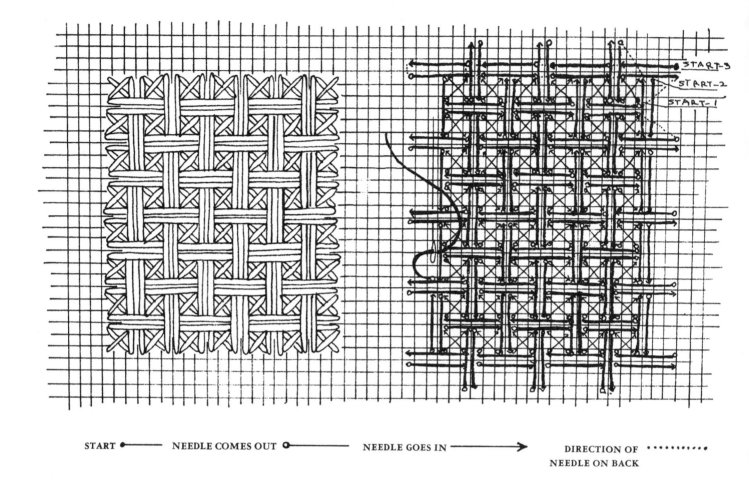

START ●————— NEEDLE COMES OUT ○————— NEEDLE GOES IN ————————▶ DIRECTION OF ·············
                                                              NEEDLE ON BACK

BUCKY'S WEAVING*

Step 1. Make diagonal crosses over 2 intersections each way over the area to be covered, leaving 1 thread between crosses and between rows. These crosses are usually done in a dark color.

Step 2. The weaving stitches are worked over 5 threads and under 1, starting at lower right leg of first cross. Make a second row directly below first on return journey. Move 1 cross stitch to the left to start next pair of rows. The third pair of rows is directly below first pair, the fourth below the second, etc.

Step 3. Starting at upper left arm of cross, and in the middle of the side of stitches of step 2, make the groups of stitches over 5 threads and under 1, vertically this time. The ends of the stitches will be hidden by stitches of step 2 and these stitches will cover the ends of the stitches of step 2, producing the effect of weaving. Heavy yarn is needed for steps 2 and 3.

* Left-handed people reverse "left" and "right."

84

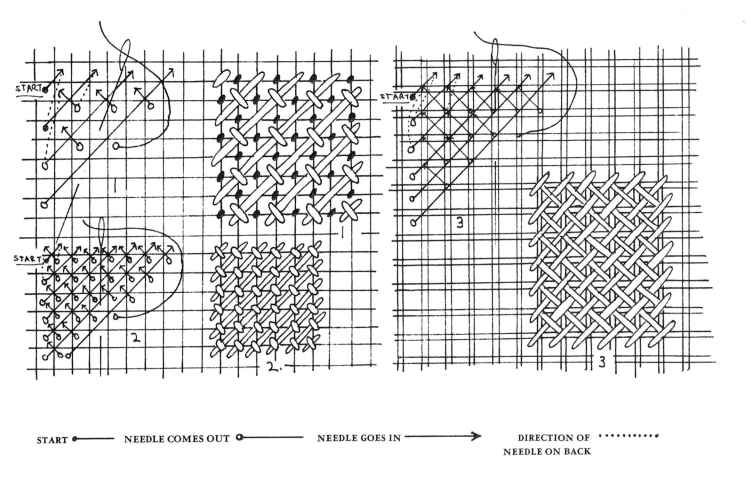

START ●——— NEEDLE COMES OUT ○———— NEEDLE GOES IN ————→ DIRECTION OF ••••••••••
                                                          NEEDLE ON BACK

WEB

This stitch pattern can be worked on both double and single mesh canvas.

1. Start with a single Tent stitch in upper left corner. Next lay a diagonal strand over 3 intersections starting 2 threads down from beginning of Tent stitch. Bring needle out 1 vertical and 2 horizontal threads down, left, and make a stitch over laid strand and 1 intersection up, left. Bring needle out 2 threads down from beginning of first laid strand and lay another strand over 5 intersections up, right. Make the short stitch over laid strand and intersection as in row 1. Make another short stitch 2 intersections down, left, bringing needle out 2 threads down from beginning of second laid strand. Continue in this manner with increasingly long laid strands and the short stitches over every other intersection and the laid strand. These stitches look like Tent stitches pointing the "wrong" way and using every other hole. Unless heavy yarn is used a pattern of intersections is left which can be covered with a Tent stitch in a contrasting color. See dots on diagram.

2. This form is really traméd Diagonal Tent stitch (p. 90). Use finer yarn. The tramé strand is laid from lower left to upper right, 1 row at a time, using every hole. All the Tent stitch rows are made from lower right to upper left with stitches pointing the "wrong" way.
   Forms 1 and 2 are similar to Bokhara Couching (p. 70), but they are made on the diagonal.

3. On double mesh canvas make a Tent stitch over 1 group of 4 intersections in upper left corner. Use the large holes for the laid strands. The shorter stitches are made diagonally across large holes from 1 small hole to another, over the laid strand. This form looks like Diagonal Weaving (p. 115). The crossing stitches will be longer than in forms 1 and 2.

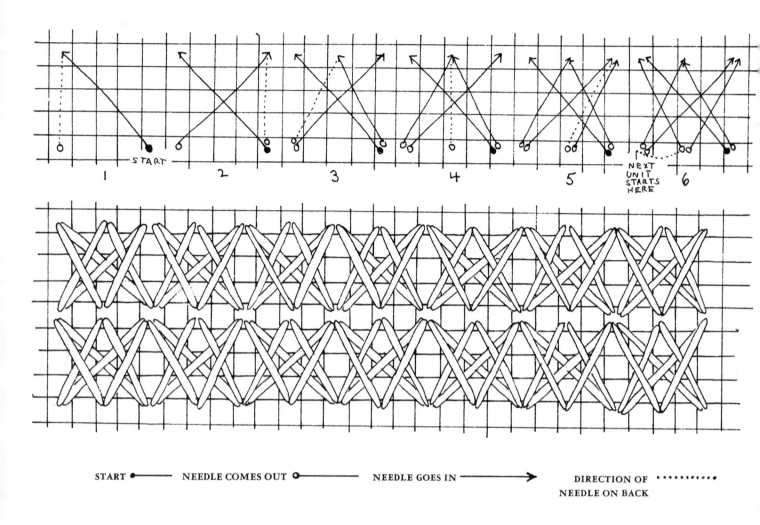

START ●——— NEEDLE COMES OUT ○——— NEEDLE GOES IN ———→ DIRECTION OF ············
NEEDLE ON BACK

TRIPLE CROSS

Start with a large cross stitch over 4 intersections each way. Then make an inverted V using same holes as bottoms of cross stitch legs and the middle hole between upper legs. Then 2 stitches forming a V, right side up, using same holes as top ends of legs of cross stitch and middle hole between bottom ends of legs. This makes 2 oblong and 1 regular crosses, 3 in all.

Follow the steps in the diagram. This pattern can be used as a wide couching. Use finer yarn.

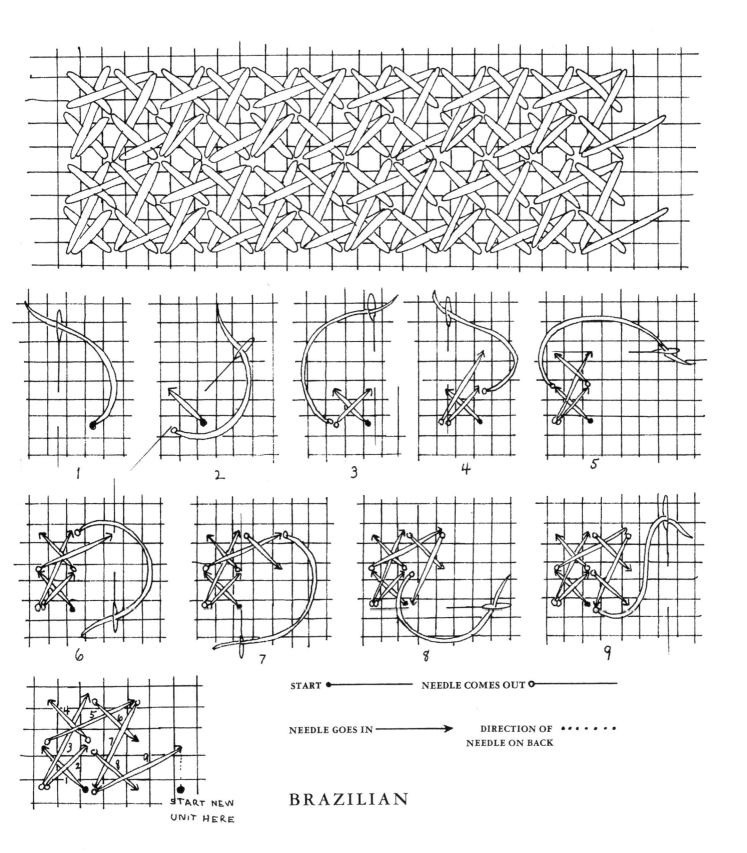

START ●——————— NEEDLE COMES OUT ○————————

NEEDLE GOES IN ——————→   DIRECTION OF •••••••
                                   NEEDLE ON BACK

START NEW
UNIT HERE

BRAZILIAN

Each stitch unit covers a 4-thread square. Follow the diagram through the 9 steps. Second unit is worked to right of first. Start all rows at left.

(Pattern researched by Bucky King.)

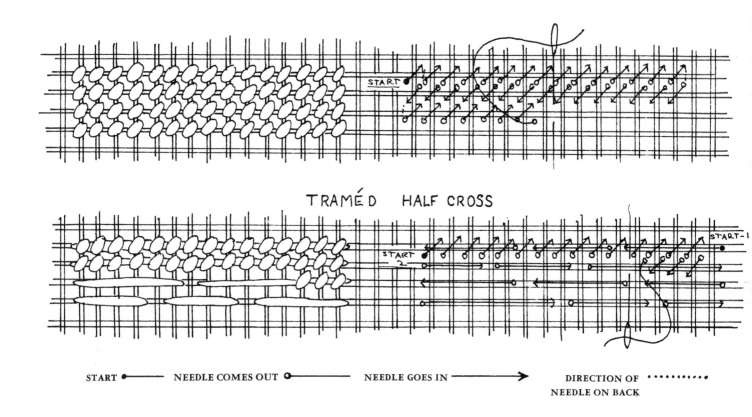

TRAMÉD HALF CROSS

START ●——— NEEDLE COMES OUT ○——— NEEDLE GOES IN ————→ DIRECTION OF ···········
NEEDLE ON BACK

HALF CROSS
Tent No. 1

The simplest form of Tent stitch, the Half Cross, can only be used on double mesh canvas. It is recommended over Continental or Diagonal where a minimum of bulk is desired. This stitch pattern *cannot* be used in quantity on single mesh canvas. Start at upper left, and with needle in a vertical position, point down, cover 1 set of intersections up, right, bringing needle out 1 set of horizontal threads down. There will be short vertical stitches on the back. In the second row needle will be in a vertical position but pointing up, away from you. If you wish, you can turn the piece half around, top at the bottom. Turn back for the third row.

Traméd Half Cross. In some commercial pieces a running strand is laid in long stitches placed between the 2 horizontal threads of 1 set of threads to indicate to worker where the different colors are to go. These strands are to be covered with a Half Cross stitch. You may place your own tramé stitches before beginning the work if you wish. Be sure to stagger the ends of stitches so one will not be under another. They can be much longer than those in the diagram. You may cover these long stitches with Continental Tent stitch if you wish, but not Diagonal Tent. The tramé strands produce a corded appearance.

88

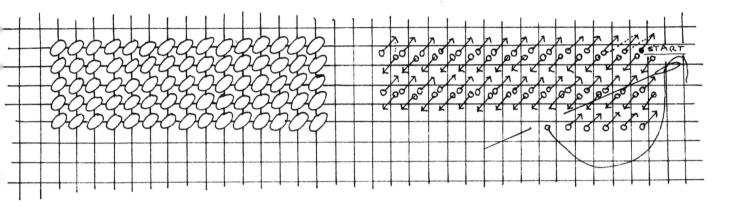

START •——— NEEDLE COMES OUT •——— NEEDLE GOES IN ———————➤ DIRECTION OF ••••••••••
                                                                        NEEDLE ON BACK

CONTINENTAL*
Tent No. 2
Horizontal

First row. Mark off with pencil area to be covered. Bring needle out in the hole at lower left of intersection in upper right corner. Insert it in upper right corner so stitch will cover intersection, and bring it out 2 threads to left and 1 thread down in the hole to the left of beginning of first stitch. Continue to the end of the row.

Second row. As you are ready to complete last stitch in row 1 bring needle out 1 thread below insertion point. Turn work around so top is at the bottom and continue as in row 1.

Third row. As you complete last stitch in the second row, with needle pointing away from you, bring it out 1 horizontal thread up or away from you. Turn work around again, and the working strand is now in position to start as in row 1.

This form of Tent stitch is popular with people who buy partially worked pieces in Penelope canvas in the shops. Its main disadvantage is that it distorts the canvas badly. Finished pieces which are to be soft, such as pillows, bags, etc., will not stay square. In time the distortion will come back. These pieces should be worked in Diagonal Tent stitch which produces almost no distortion.

---

* Left-handed people turn diagram halfway around (top at bottom) and start in lower left corner.

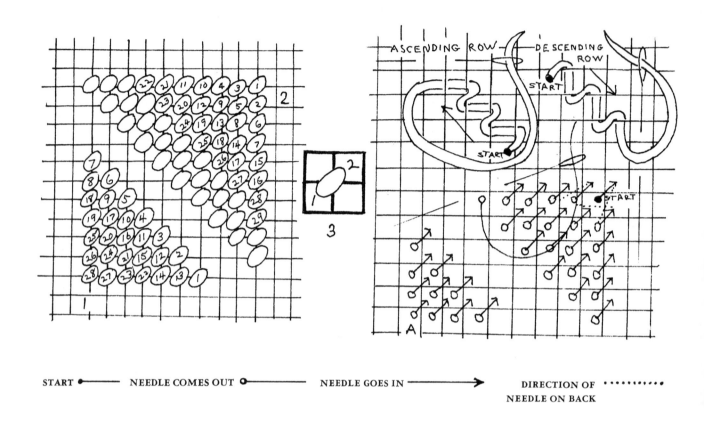

START ●————— NEEDLE COMES OUT ○————— NEEDLE GOES IN ————→ DIRECTION OF ••••••••••
NEEDLE ON BACK

DIAGONAL TENT*
Tent No. 3

If you follow the three steps in this important basic stitch pattern, you will not find it hard to master. First study the two basic row patterns at top of right diagram. Note how needle is held straight up and down and passes under 2 horizontal threads on downward journey. The needle is held straight across and passes under 2 vertical threads on upward journey. The stitch is made over 1 intersection of canvas threads. This is true of all forms of Tent stitch. Next work a triangle, starting with the diagonal side and ending with a single stitch (1).

Now work a triangle, starting in the corner with a single stitch (2). Follow the numbered stitches in the diagram.

One rule to remember is that there are 4 holes around each intersection. In all forms of Tent stitch, the needle always comes out in the lower left hole and goes in in the upper right as in diagram 3.

For further particulars on the use of this stitch pattern, see "Diagonal Tent Stitch—Some Dos and Don'ts, Some Hints and Tricks," by Katharine Ireys.

* Left-handed people turn diagram halfway around (top at bottom) and start in lower left corner.

90

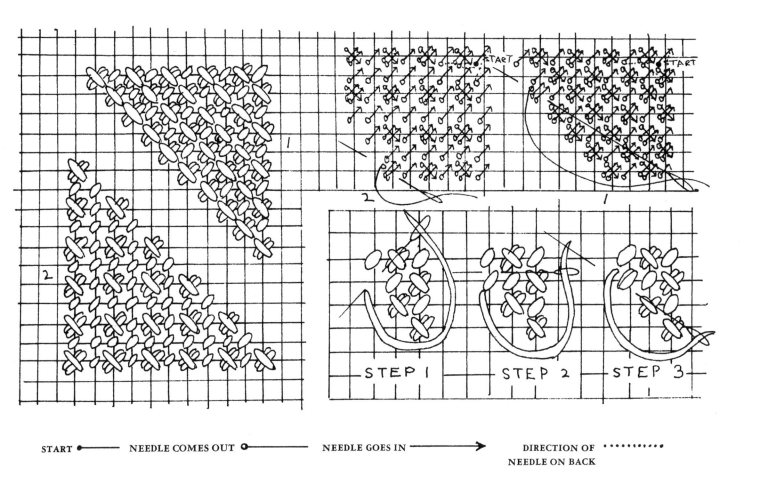

HOBNAIL 1 & 2*

1. This stitch pattern is a variation of Diagonal Tent stitch (p. 90). Rows from upper left to lower right (with needle in vertical position) are worked in plain Tent stitch. The rows from lower right to upper left are worked as follows: Make a Tent stitch in the usual manner but bring needle out at beginning of stitch so as to put a second stitch on top of the first one (step 1). Insert needle in same hole as end of first stitch and bring it out 1 thread to the left (step 2). Make a diagonal stitch down, right, crossing the first 2 stitches, and bringing it out for beginning of next Hobnail stitch (step 3). This makes a small cross stitch on top of regular Tent stitch, 3 thicknesses of yarn in one place, producing the little bump. Finish the row in this manner. Alternate these rows with rows of plain Diagonal Tent stitch.

2. In version 2, the ascending row alternates Hobnail stitches with plain.

The Hobnails can be made in a contrasting color by covering the area with plain Tent and then placing the little crosses over evenly spaced stitches. For versions 1 and 2, use finer yarn than you would use for regular Tent stitch.

* Left-handed people turn diagram halfway around (top at bottom) and start in lower left corner.

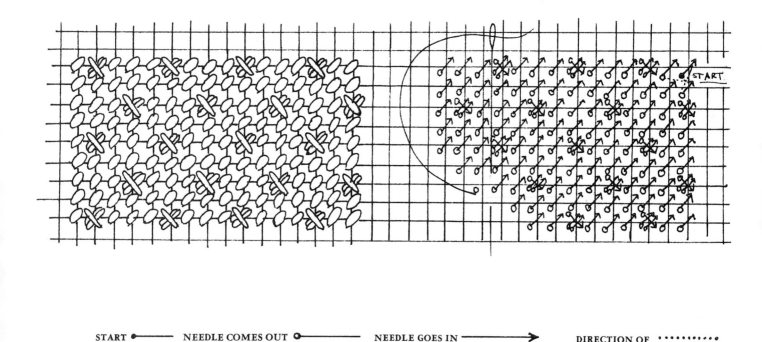

DOTTED SWISS*
Hobnail 3

This version of Hobnail has more widely spaced Hobnail stitches. They are usually made in a contrasting color. The little crosses are made on every other ascending row, every other stitch. This pattern looks like the fabric called Dotted Swiss.

* Left-handed people turn diagram halfway around (top at bottom) and start in lower left corner.

92

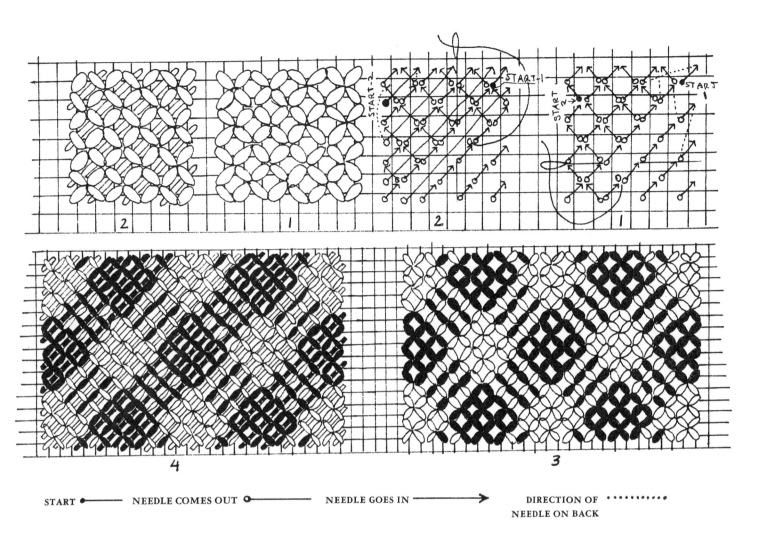

START ●——— NEEDLE COMES OUT ⊶——— NEEDLE GOES IN ———→ DIRECTION OF ·············
                                                       NEEDLE ON BACK

ALTERNATING TENT*

1. Work every other row in Diagonal Tent stitch (p. 90). Turn work one-fourth way around and fill in with stitches pointing in the opposite direction. Unless yarn matches canvas heavy yarn is needed.

2. Work step 1 as in diagram 1. Now starting in the upper left corner, lay a strand between rows of stitches and pointing in the same direction as stitches of step 1. Lay 1 strand at a time and cover with Tent stitches on return journey before laying next strand. Because the laid strand helps to cover the canvas, finer yarn must be used for step 2.

3 and 4. Diagrams 3 and 4 are striped diagonally, forming check patterns. Unfortunately pen and ink diagrams fail to show the charm or the possibilities of this stitch pattern. Many versions are possible, even Scotch tartans.

* Left-handed people turn diagram halfway around (top at bottom) and start in lower left corner.

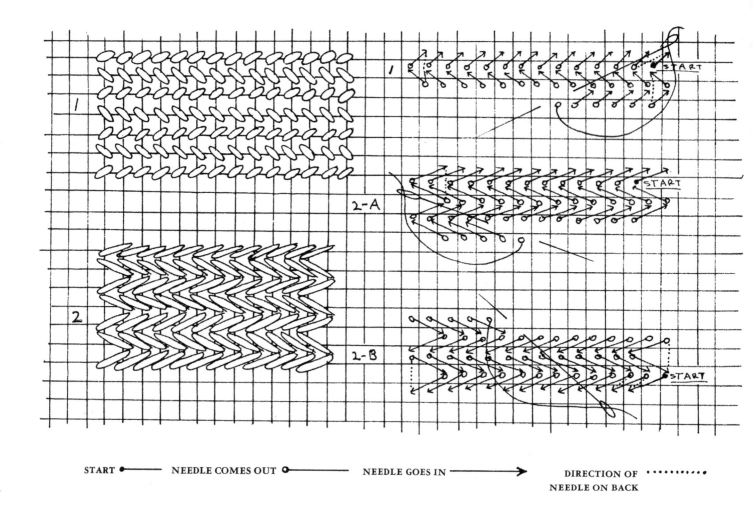

START ●——— NEEDLE COMES OUT ○——————— NEEDLE GOES IN ⟶ DIRECTION OF •••••••••
NEEDLE ON BACK

REVERSE TENT 1 & 2

1. Work a series of Tent stitches in a horizontal row from right to left over 1 intersection each, like Continental Tent (p. 89). In the second row, worked from left to right, the stitch direction is reversed. The third row repeats row 1, the fourth row 2, etc.

2. The stitches are similar to Reverse Tent 1 except that they cover 1 horizontal and 2 vertical threads, making a greater slant and a longer stitch. It can be worked two ways:

2A. The stitch can be started at its left end, with the needle passing under 3 vertical and 1 horizontal threads down, left.

2B. Start at bottom of area to be covered. Bring needle out at right end of stitch, and insert it 2 vertical and 1 horizontal threads down, left. Bring it out 1 intersection up, right and repeat. This method is used when method 2A crowds the canvas, distorting the threads. It uses less yarn. The back looks like Reverse Tent 1.

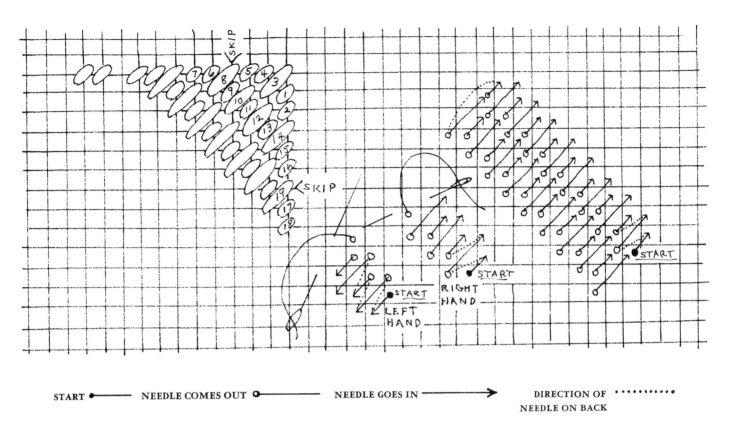

START ●——— NEEDLE COMES OUT ⊙——— NEEDLE GOES IN ⟶ DIRECTION OF •••••••••
NEEDLE ON BACK

DIAGONAL PARISIAN*
DIAGONAL FLORENTINE
Florence

Long and short stitches cover 1 intersection, 2 intersections, 1, 2, 1, etc. The long stitches of row 2 fit up to the short stitches of row 1, and vice versa.

Because straight edges are hard to achieve, it is a good idea to start with a row across the middle of the area to be covered. Work to bottom, left,* compensating along the sides as you go. Now turn work halfway around (top to bottom) and work to bottom, left* again.

Be careful not to pull your stitches too tight, as this pattern will warp the canvas badly.

Straight edges. Follow numbered stitches in the diagram at left. Remember to put 2 short stitches at the end of each row, skip 1 thread, and start new row with 2 short stitches. The skipped thread will be covered by your first long stitch.

* Left-handed people work to upper right, turn work halfway around, and work to upper right again. For straight edges, turn diagram halfway around and start in lower left corner.

95

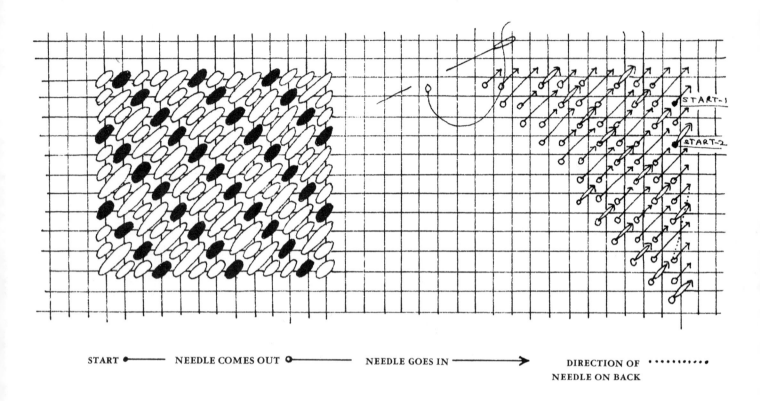

START ●————— NEEDLE COMES OUT ○————— NEEDLE GOES IN ————→ DIRECTION OF •••••••••
                                                            NEEDLE ON BACK

DIAGONAL PARISIAN & TENT*

This stitch pattern consists of rows of Diagonal Parisian (Diagonal Florentine) (p. 95) alternating with rows of Diagonal Tent stitch (p. 90). The Tent stitches are placed next to the short stitches of the Diagonal Parisian. It is a good idea to carry both stitch patterns along together to avoid getting mixed up at the ends of rows. If worked separately, remember to skip an extra thread at the ends of rows of Diagonal Parisian to allow for the Tent stitches. If the Tent stitch is in place at the end of the row, skip 1 thread beyond it, then put in 2 short stitches of Diagonal Parisian, then the long stitch, and proceed with the row. Remember to put 2 short stitches at the end of the row.

It is best to be familiar with Diagonal Parisian before trying this combination.

* Left-handed people turn diagram halfway around (top at bottom) and start in lower left corner.

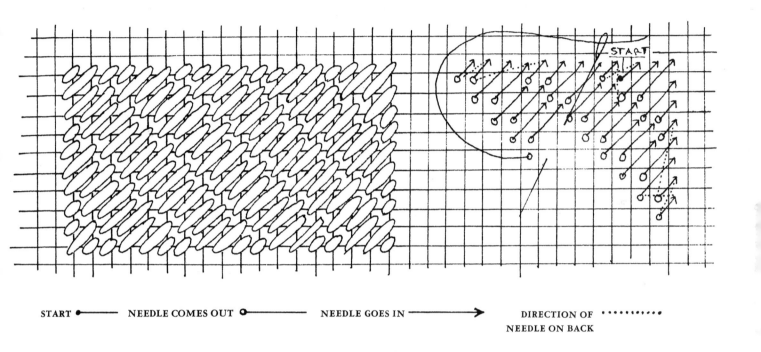

START ●————— NEEDLE COMES OUT ◦————— NEEDLE GOES IN ——————→ DIRECTION OF ●●●●●●●●●●
                                                                NEEDLE ON BACK

LONG DIAGONAL*

This is diagonal rows of diagonal stitches covering 2 intersections each. Edges of rows are stepped in a zigzag. The procedure for producing straight edges is similar to that of Diagonal Parisian (Florentine) (p. 95). Finish row with 2 Tent stitches, skip 2 threads, and then make 2 more Tent stitches along the edge. The first 2 long stitches of row will fill the gap.

This stitch pattern could be called a variation of Byzantine (p. 109), which is really Florentine on the diagonal.

* Left-handed people turn diagram halfway around (top at bottom) and start in lower left corner.

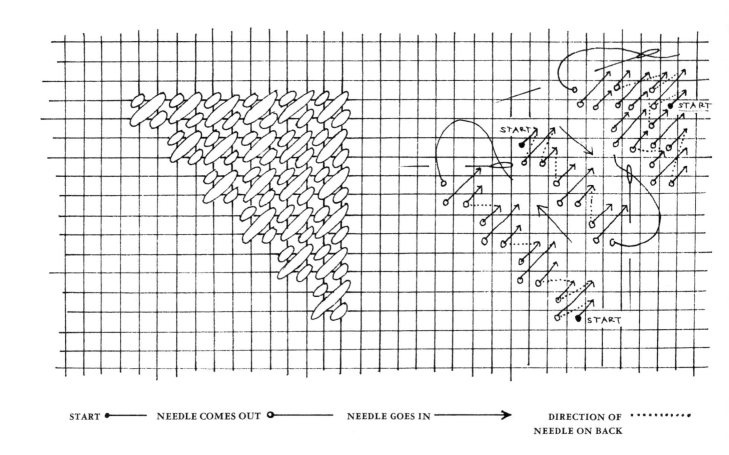

START ●——— NEEDLE COMES OUT ○——— NEEDLE GOES IN ———▶ DIRECTION OF ••••••••••
NEEDLE ON BACK

MOSAIC*

Practice single diagonal rows, both up and down, before trying to work a corner. Notice that on the descending row the needle is held vertically and passes under 2 threads between units. In the ascending row the needle is held horizontally and again passes under 2 threads between units. The units consist of 3 stitches each, over 1, 2, 1 intersections, forming little squares. When starting in a corner notice that you skip 1 thread before starting a new row.

The little squares created by this pattern look like small mosaic tiles, which is the reason for the name.

* Left-handed people turn diagram halfway around (top at bottom) and start in lower left corner.

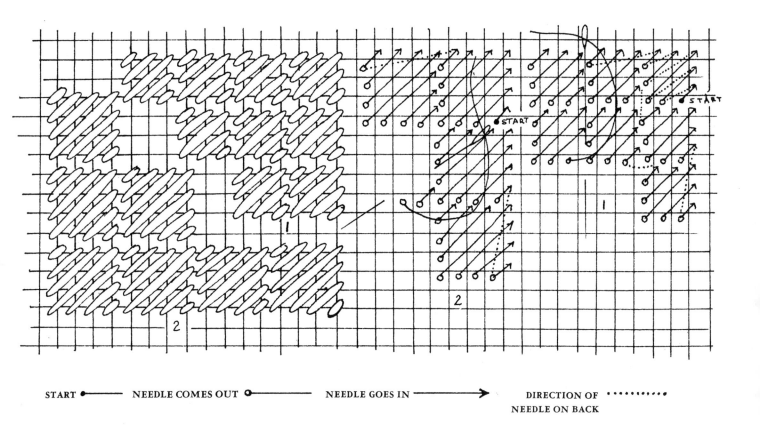

START •——— NEEDLE COMES OUT ○——— NEEDLE GOES IN ———→   DIRECTION OF •••••••••
                                                                     NEEDLE ON BACK

DIAGONAL SATIN*

1. Start 3 threads down on right side of area to be covered. Make a series of diagonal stitches over 1, 2, 3, 2, 1 intersections slanting up, right, forming a square over 3 threads each way. Bring needle out 4 threads to left and 1 thread down. Now make 2 squares starting at top left corner, 1 to left of first square and 1 below. Bring needle out 4 threads down and 1 thread to the left. Make a diagonal row of 3 squares, starting each square in the lower right corner. Continue making diagonal rows in this manner.

2. This version is essentially the same as version 1 except the square units cover 4 threads each way. Each unit is composed of 7 stitches covering 1, 2, 3, 4, 3, 2, 1 intersections.

Care should be taken to keep stitches fairly loose to avoid warping canvas and leaving exposed threads between squares. If desired, Back stitches (p. 137) can be placed between squares.

* Left-handed people turn diagram halfway around (top at the bottom) and start in lower left corner.

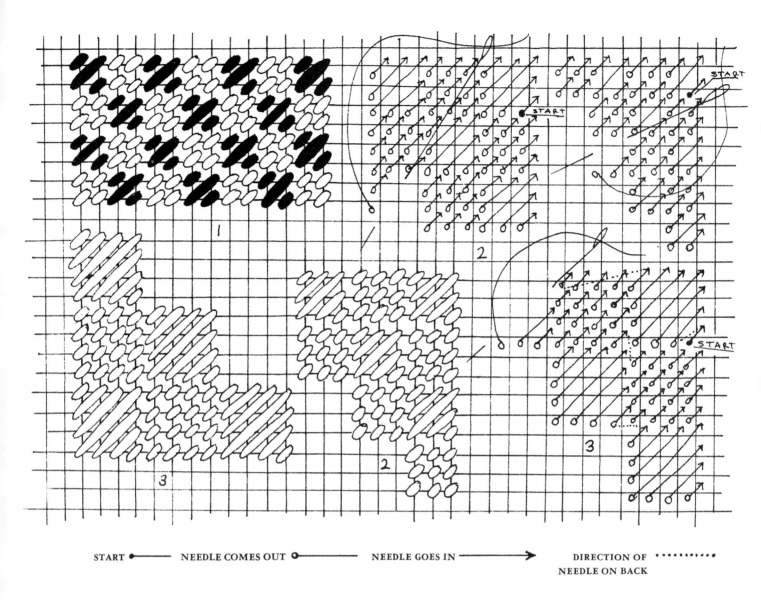

START •———— NEEDLE COMES OUT O———— NEEDLE GOES IN ——————➤ DIRECTION OF •••••••••
NEEDLE ON BACK

CHECKER 1, 2, & 3*

This stitch pattern is really a composite of Diagonal Satin (p. 99) and Diagonal Tent stitch (p. 90) arranged in a checker pattern.

1. This version uses units of Mosaic (p. 98), which is the smallest form of Diagonal Satin, alternating with squares of 4 Tent stitches.

2. This version uses units of 3-thread square Diagonal Satin and squares of 9 Tent stitch.

3. This version uses units of Diagonal Satin covering 4 threads each way and 16 stitch square of Tent.

When made in one color, work in diagonal rows. Make a row of Diagonal Satin and then a row of Tent stitch squares, completing each square of Tent as you go along. If contrasting colors are desired, work one part and fill in with the other.

* Left-handed people turn work halfway around (top at bottom) and start in lower left corner.

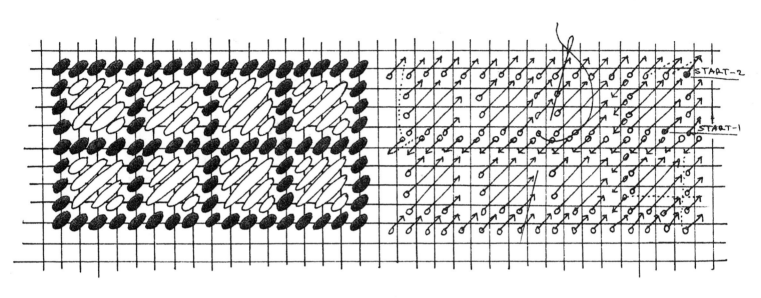

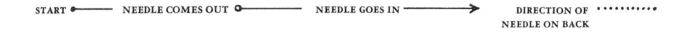

START •———— NEEDLE COMES OUT O————— NEEDLE GOES IN ——————▶ DIRECTION OF • • • • • • • • • •
                                                                           NEEDLE ON BACK

SCOTCH*
Scottish

A composite of Diagonal Satin and Continental Tent stitches (see pp. 89 and 99).

Step 1. Starting at lower right corner, work 3-thread squares of Diagonal Satin in horizontal rows, leaving 1 thread between squares and rows.

Step 2. These are to be covered with Continental Tent stitches. Work the horizontal rows first, then the vertical. Be careful not to reverse direction of Tent stitches. The Tent stitches are usually done in a contrasting color.

For large areas, the direction of the stitches of step 1 can be reversed in alternating squares, as in Flat stitch (p. 102). This will prevent distortion.

* Left-handed people turn diagram halfway around (top at bottom) and start in lower left corner.

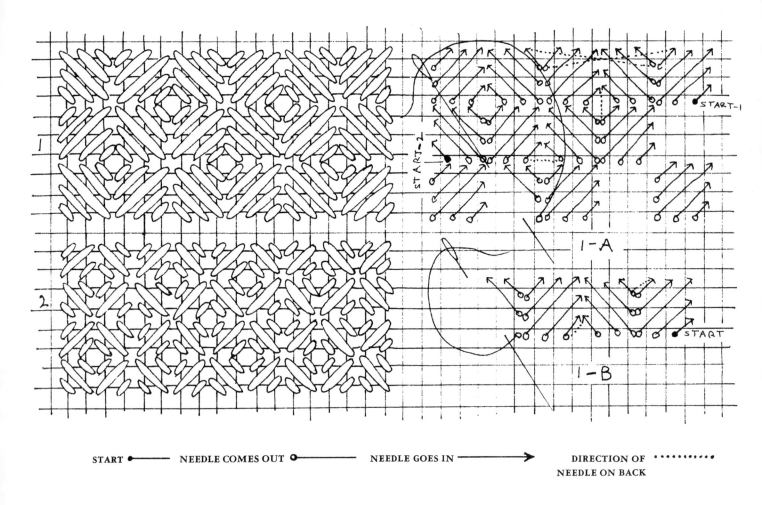

START ●━━━━ NEEDLE COMES OUT ◦━━━━ NEEDLE GOES IN ━━━━▶ DIRECTION OF ••••••••• NEEDLE ON BACK

FLAT 1 & 2

1A. This stitch pattern is made up of squares of diagonal stitches over 1, 2, 3, 2, 1 intersections.

   Step 1.   Work squares in diagonal rows, every other row, all stitches pointing in one direction to form a checkerboard.

   Step 2.   Turn work one-fourth way around and fill in intervening squares with stitches pointing in the opposite direction. This is much like the Cushion No. 2 (p. 104) but without the laid strand under step 2.

1B. If you like, this stitch pattern may be worked in horizontal rows, changing the direction of the stitches for each unit.

2. This is a smaller version, the stitches covering 1, 2, 1 intersections per unit. You have the same choice of direction of rows as in the first version. This pattern is related to Mosaic (p. 98). It is sometimes called Alternating Mosaic.

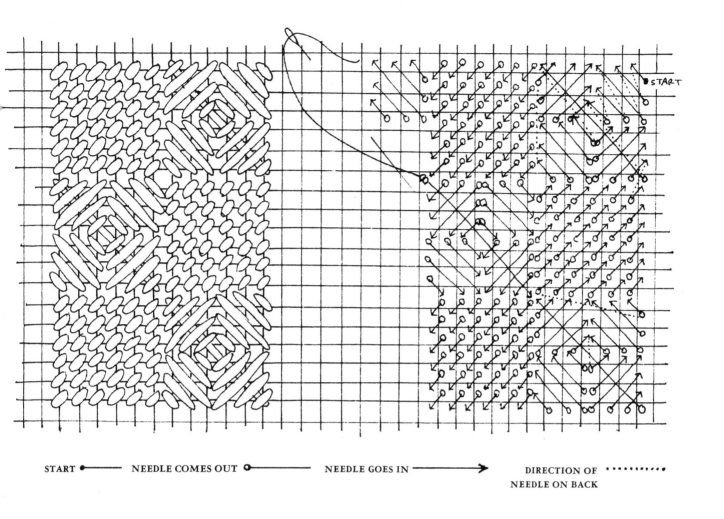

START ●——— NEEDLE COMES OUT ○——— NEEDLE GOES IN ——————→ DIRECTION OF •••••••••
NEEDLE ON BACK

CUSHION 1*

Work diagonal stitches over a three-thread square, covering 1, 2, 3, 2, 1 intersections. Bring needle out 3 threads down from beginning of longest stitch. Insert needle 6 intersections diagonally up, left, or 3 threads to left of end of longest stitch. Bring needle out diagonally 1 intersection down, left, from beginning of fifth or shortest stitch. Then make another 3-thread square diagonally down, left, from the first one. Now bring needle out 1 thread down from end of your long stitch. Work diagonal stitches slanting in the opposite direction over the two three-thread squares covering the long stitch. Work these units in a checkerboard with Diagonal Tent (p. 90). The cushion units can be worked first in a checker pattern, from upper right to lower left. Fill in the six-thread squares that are left with Diagonal Tent.

If you wish to use the Cushion stitch units by themselves, see Cushion 2 which follows.

* Left-handed people turn diagram halfway around (top at bottom) and start in lower left corner.

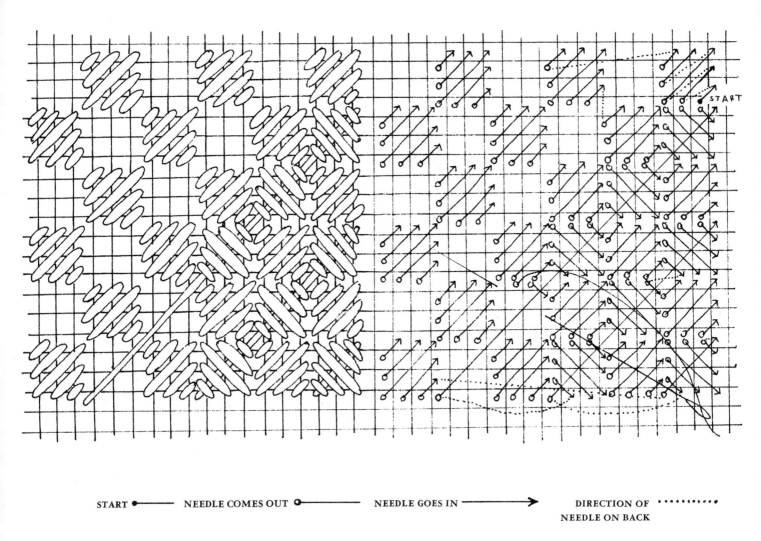

START •——— NEEDLE COMES OUT •———— NEEDLE GOES IN ————▶ DIRECTION OF •••••••••••
NEEDLE ON BACK

CUSHION 2*

Step 1. Work diagonal stitches over 3-thread squares in diagonal rows, covering 1, 2, 3, 2, 1 intersections in a checker-board pattern over the entire area, leaving the intervening squares unworked.

Step 2. Lay a long stitch pointing in the *same* direction as the stitches of step 1 diagonally over a row of vacant squares. Pass the needle under 1 thread and work diagonal stitches over 1, 2, 3, 2, 1 intersections slanting in the *opposite* direction over the row of vacant squares, covering the long laid stitch and using the same holes as step 1. Work the rest of the rows in this manner.

This form of Cushion stitch is used where a large area is to be covered.

* Left-handed people turn diagram halfway around (top at bottom) and start in lower left corner.

104

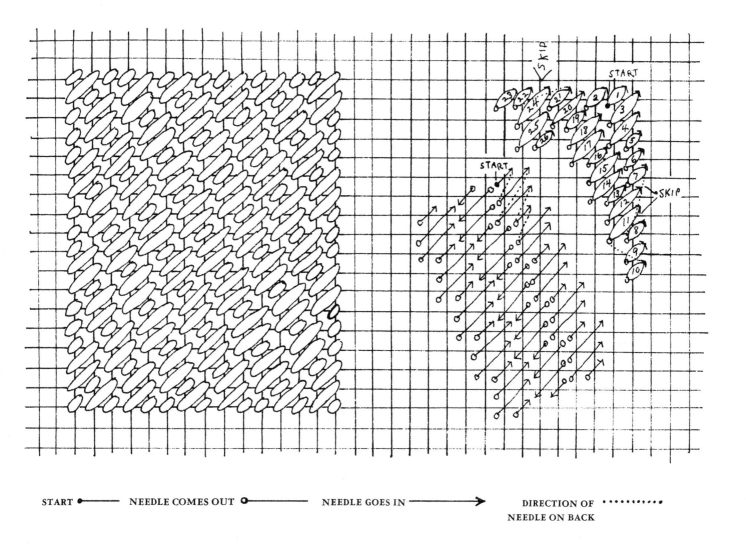

START •——— NEEDLE COMES OUT ⊶——— NEEDLE GOES IN ————➤ DIRECTION OF •••••••••
NEEDLE ON BACK

CASHMERE 1

This stitch pattern is related to Diagonal Parisian (Florentine) (p. 95). There are 2 long stitches, one below the other, between short stitches instead of 1. The progression is short, long, long, short, long, long, short. The rows slant down to the right but not diagonally.

The simplest way to fit this stitch pattern into a space is to work a row across the largest area. Work to bottom of the area, compensating at edges as you go. Now turn work halfway around (top at bottom), and work to the bottom again. Use this method even for a rectangular shape, as compensating for straight edges is complicated.

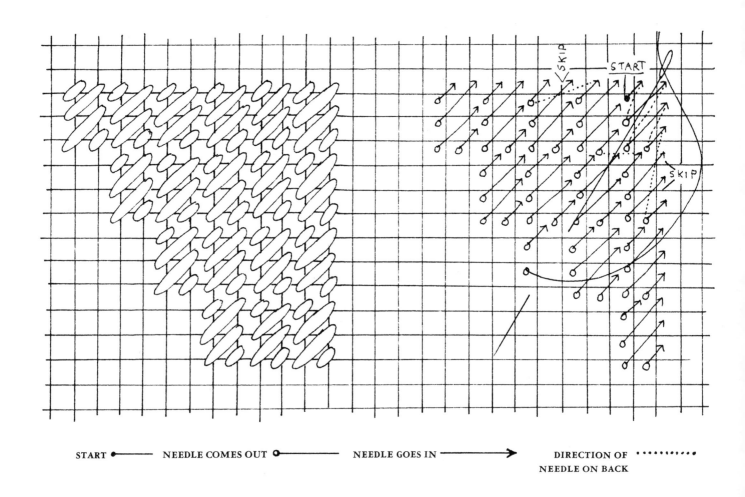

START ●———— NEEDLE COMES OUT O———— NEEDLE GOES IN ————▶ DIRECTION OF ● ● ● ● ● ● ● ● ●
                                                        NEEDLE ON BACK

CASHMERE 2*

This stitch is related to Mosaic (p. 98). There are two long stitches, one under the other, instead of one in each unit. The progression of stitches is short, long, long, short—short, long, long, short, etc. The rows slant down, right, but not diagonally. The stitch units form little oblongs beside and under each other.

* Left-handed people turn diagram halfway around (top at the bottom) and start at lower left corner.

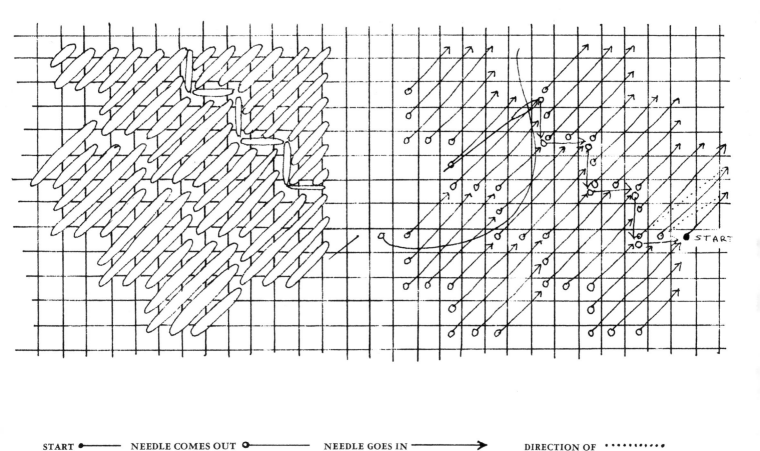

START •——— NEEDLE COMES OUT o——— NEEDLE GOES IN ———⟶ DIRECTION OF •••••••••
NEEDLE ON BACK

DIAGONAL*

Diagonal stitch covers 2, 3, 4, 3, 2, 3, 4, etc., intersections. The longest stitches on second row fit up to shortest stitches of first row. Back stitches covering 2 threads can be placed between rows. The diagram on the left shows compensation for straight edges; the one on the right does not.

* Left-handed people turn diagram halfway around (top at bottom) and start in lower left corner.

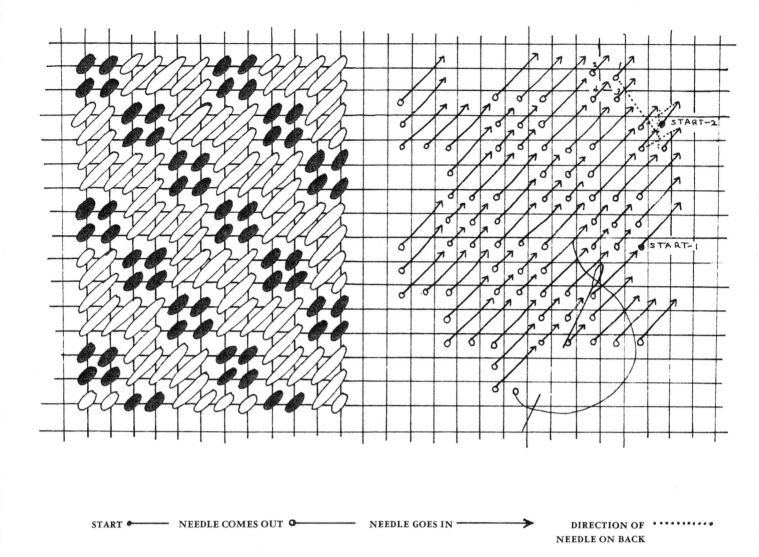

START ●——— NEEDLE COMES OUT ○——— NEEDLE GOES IN ————▶ DIRECTION OF ••••••••••
NEEDLE ON BACK

DIAGONAL HUNGARIAN GROUND*

Make a diagonal row of diagonal stitches over 2 intersections each. The row zigzags in steps in groups of 3's (counting the corner twice). The second row is arranged so as to leave squares of 4 intersections each between rows. Bring points of steps together. Fill in the 4 intersection squares with Tent stitch, usually in a contrasting color. If you wish, a Mosaic stitch unit (p. 98) may be substituted for the 4 Tent stitches. Diagram 1 shows compensation for straight edges.

* Left-handed people turn diagram halfway around (top at bottom) and start in lower left corner.

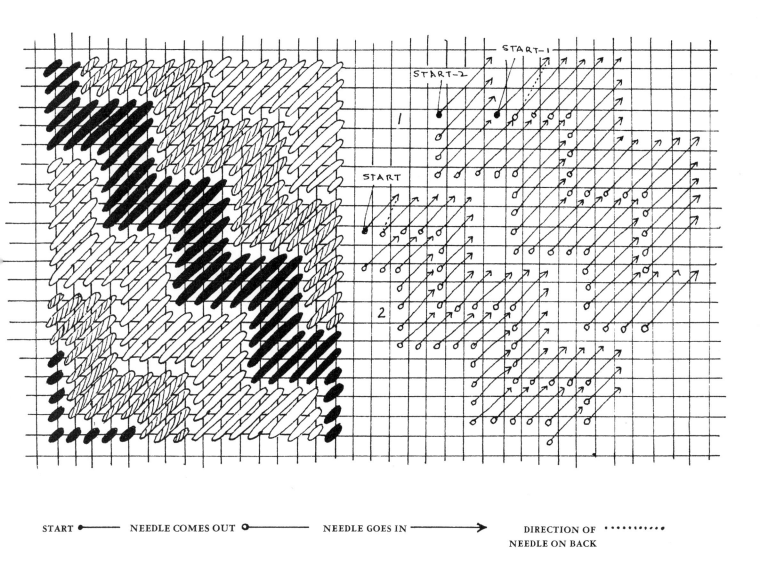

BYZANTINE*

Byzantine is really a diagonal form of simple Florentine (p. 12). Diagonal rows of diagonal stitches are arranged in a zig-zag, a constant number of stitches to each step. Diagrams 1 and 2 show 5 stitches to a step (counting the corner stitch twice). As many as 8 or 9 can be used. Diagram 1 shows stitches covering 3 intersections. Using different values of one color, as in Florentine, produces a pleasing effect. Diagram 2 shows stitches covering 2 intersections, which is the minimum number possible. This form, using one color, makes a good background. Care should be taken to leave the stitches fairly loose as this stitch pattern warps the canvas badly. The diagram at left shows compensation for straight edges.

* Left-handed people turn diagram halfway around (top at bottom) and start in lower left corner.

109

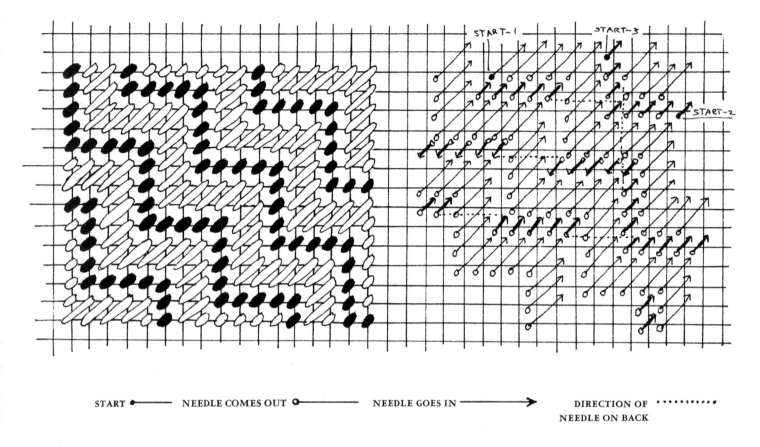

START ●——— NEEDLE COMES OUT ○——— NEEDLE GOES IN ———→ DIRECTION OF ⋯⋯⋯⋯
NEEDLE ON BACK

JACQUARD*

Step 1. Work diagonal stitches over 2 intersections in zigzag rows, 5 stitches each way (counting the corner twice, once for each way). Leave 1 thread between rows for Continental Tent stitch (p. 89) fill-in in a contrasting color.

Step 2. It would seem logical to work the Tent stitch following the zigs and zags of step 1, but in order to do so, you would have to "backtrack." This would mean using Half Cross Tent, which doesn't work well on single mesh canvas. The problem is solved by working all horizontal groups first, stepping across under the long stitches. Work all 5 stitches in each group. Then, working vertically, fill in the 3 remaining stitches. The diagram looks complicated, but you will find this quite easy to do. If you wish, you can work the Tent stitches pointing the other way. Then there is no problem. This pattern is effective when it is done in one color.

* Left-handed people turn diagram halfway around (top at bottom) and start at lower left corner.

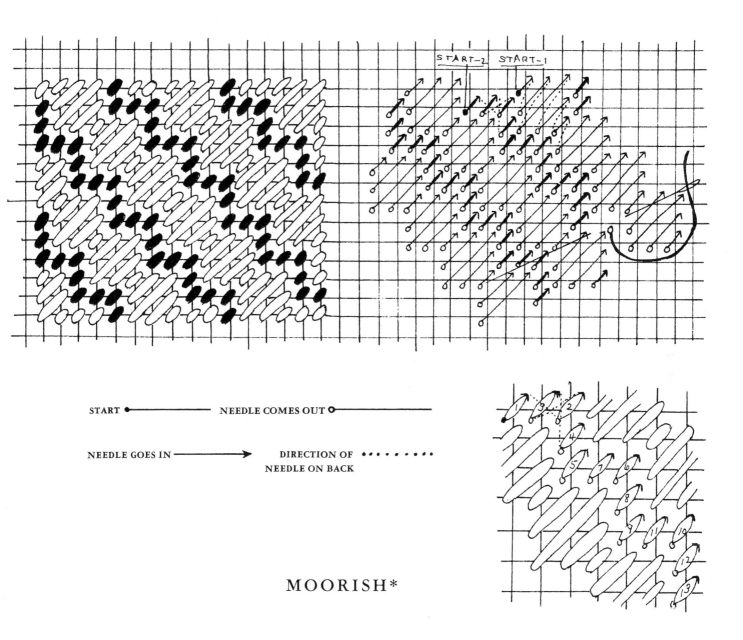

START ●————————— NEEDLE COMES OUT ○—————————

NEEDLE GOES IN ——————▶ DIRECTION OF • • • • • • •
NEEDLE ON BACK

MOORISH*

Work diagonal stitches in diagonal rows covering 1, 2, 3, 2, 1, 2, 3, etc., intersections. Leave 1 thread between rows. The long stitches of second row fit up to short stitches of first row and vice versa.

It would seem logical to follow the zigzag spaces for the Tent stitch fill-in, but to do so you would be using Half Cross for two of the stitches in the horizontal row, which doesn't work well on single mesh canvas. So follow the numbers on the small diagram and all the stitches will stay in place.

For a variation of this stitch pattern, eliminate the Tent stitch rows. Work the rows of step 1 next to each other.

* Left-handed people turn diagram halfway around (top at bottom) and start in lower left corner.

111

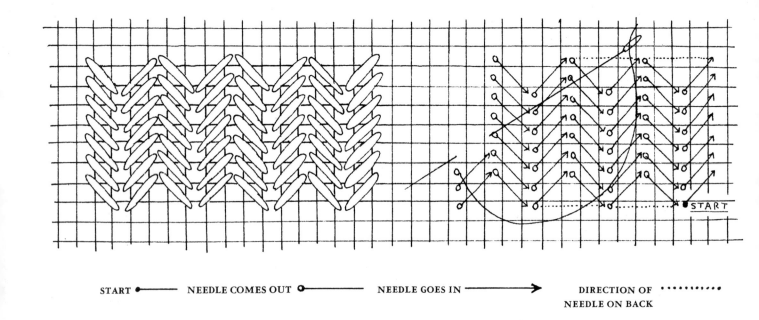

START ●———— NEEDLE COMES OUT ○———— NEEDLE GOES IN ————▶ DIRECTION OF ••••••••••
NEEDLE ON BACK

KNITTING 2*

Work diagonal stitches in vertical rows, covering 2 intersections each. Ascending row—lower left to upper right; descending row—upper left to lower right.

This stitch pattern is somewhat similar to Stem except that every hole is used and no Back stitches (p. 137) are added.

* Left-handed people reverse "left" and "right."

112

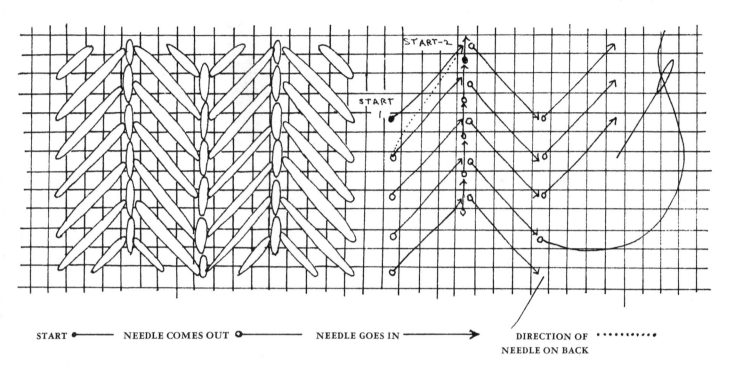

START ●━━━ NEEDLE COMES OUT O━━○ NEEDLE GOES IN ━━━━▶ DIRECTION OF ● ● ● ● ● ● ● ●
NEEDLE ON BACK

STEM*

This stitch can be worked over any number of intersections in vertical rows using every other hole, and alternating direction of stitches in each row. Back stitches are worked over exposed threads covering 2 threads with each stitch. Use the same color or a contrasting one. Heavy yarn is needed to cover canvas.

* Left-handed people reverse "left" and "right."

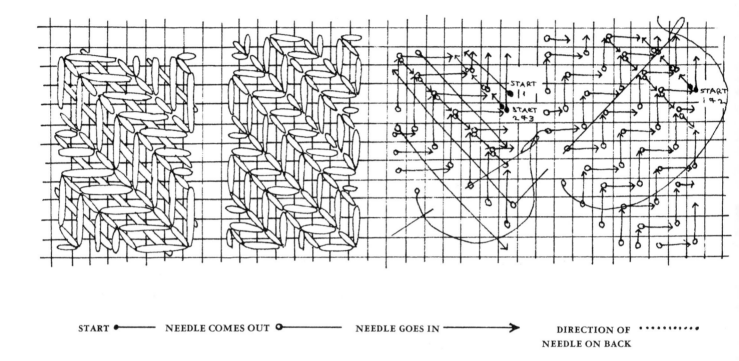

START ●━━━ NEEDLE COMES OUT ○━━━ NEEDLE GOES IN ━━━━▶ DIRECTION OF ••••••••••
NEEDLE ON BACK

DIAGONAL STEM*

Work a diagonal row of vertical stitches covering 2 or 3 threads. In the second row make horizontal stitches over 2 or 3 threads. Alternate these two rows. A tramé strand may be used if desired. Work Back stitches (p. 137) between rows in the same or a contrasting color. Diagrams show some compensation.

* Left-handed people turn diagram halfway around (top at bottom) and start in lower left corner.

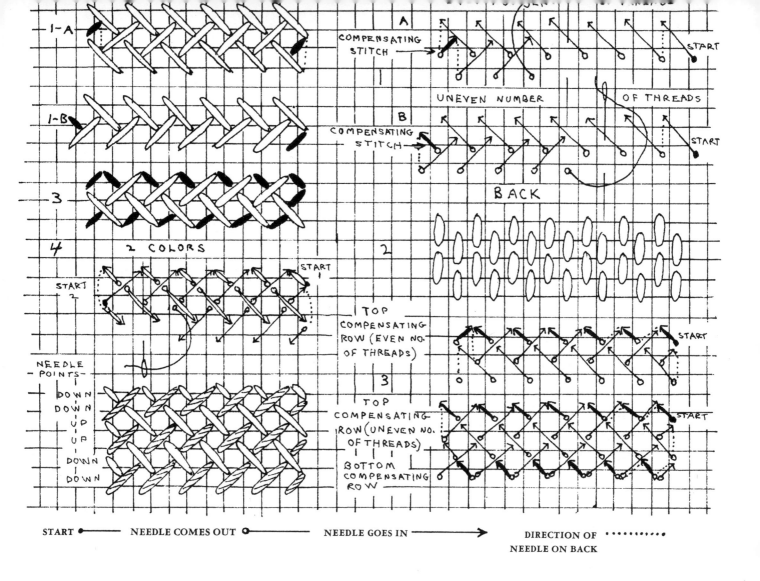

DIAGONAL WEAVING

This stitch pattern is made up of diagonal stitches over 2 intersections, slanting up, left, and up, right, in alternating rows. The main thing to remember is that the needle passes under 2 threads for *every stitch,* even when a compensating stitch is made at the beginning or end of a row. The back of the work, diagram 2, looks like small size Bricking (p. 2).

In diagram 1-A (even number of threads) there is a compensating stitch at the beginning of row 2, worked from left to right. This is really the top half of a full stitch. Pass the needle under 2 threads and you are in position to work row 2. There will be a compensating stitch at the end of row 2, which is the bottom half of a full stitch. Again pass the needle under 2 threads, and you are in position to start row 3, which has no compensating stitches. Rows 2, 4, 6, worked from left to right, have compensating stitches at both ends. Rows 1, 3, 5, etc. have no compensating stitches.

In diagram 1-B (uneven number of threads) there are compensating stitches at the ends of all rows. These are the bottom halves of full stitches.

Diagram 3 shows compensating stitches along the top and bottom edges. The top one is worked in place of regular row 1.

In diagram 4 alternating rows are worked in contrasting colors. Keep 2 needles threaded, and work the 2 colored rows as you go along. In half of the rows, the needle will be inserted at the bottom of the stitch and come out at the top.

This stitch pattern has the advantage of looking the same when viewed from the top, bottom, or sides. However, it is not a good idea to change the direction of the rows from horizontal to vertical in a single piece. Because the stitches on the back are all in one direction, they will shorten the piece slightly when used over a large area.

115

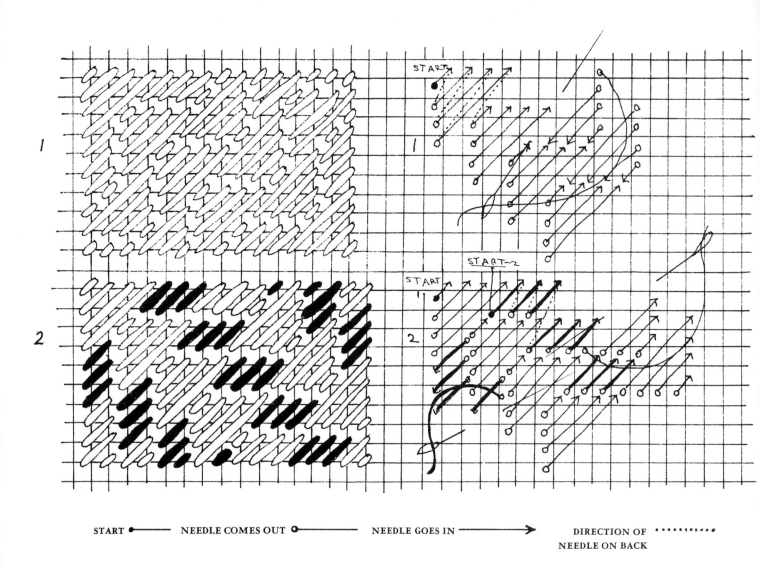

START ●——— NEEDLE COMES OUT ○——— NEEDLE GOES IN ——————▶ DIRECTION OF ·············
NEEDLE ON BACK

ORIENTAL 1 & 2
Milanese

The basic stitch pattern starts in upper left corner and covers 1, 2, 3, 4 intersections, starting again with 1. Rows go down, right, forming little triangles. In Oriental 1, the second row is reversed so triangles fit together. Make the shortest stitch next to longest one and vice versa.

Oriental 1 is sometimes called Milanese. The stitch pattern is the same on the surface, but is produced differently. Each row is a series of Back stitches slanting diagonally down, left, or up, right. The stitches cover 4, 1, 4, 1, 4, etc., intersections in the first row, 3, 2, 3, 2, 3 in the second row, 2, 3, 2, 3, 2 in the third, and 1, 4, 1, 4, 1 in the fourth. This method warps the canvas badly.

In Oriental 2, the rows are spread apart so that the longest stitches come next to each other. Fill in with Slanted Gobelin (p. 22) over 2 intersections in a contrasting color.

116

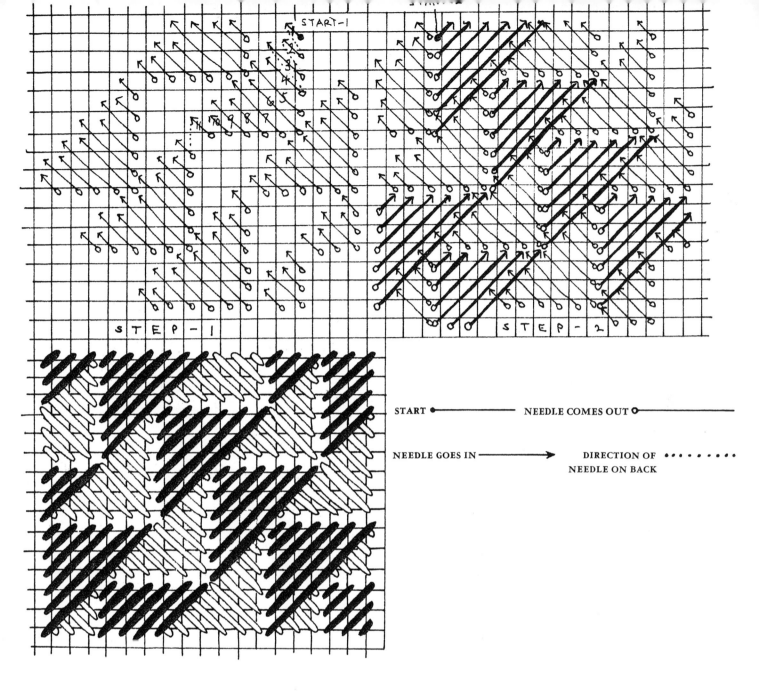

START ●———————— NEEDLE COMES OUT ⟀

NEEDLE GOES IN ————————→   DIRECTION OF ● ● ● ● ● ● ● ●
                              NEEDLE ON BACK

ORIENTAL VARIATION

Step 1. Work rows of diagonal stitches slanting from lower right to upper left, forming triangles. Cover 1 intersection (1), then another directly below (2). Now 2 stitches covering 2 intersections each (3, 4), lined up on right side with 1 and 2. Now 2 stitches covering 3, lined up on the right side with the other stitches (5, 6). Now make a stitch covering 3 but beginning 1 hole to the left of beginning of stitch 6 (7). Then 2 2's and 2 1's lined up along the bottom. Eleven stitches in all form a triangle. The diagonal side of the triangle is stepped down in a zigzag. Continue these triangles across the area down, left. Line up rows by counting intersections down, right, or up, left. The first stitch of the triangle covers the third intersection down, right, or up, left, so that stitches 5, 6, and 7 are touching in common holes.

Step 2. Beginning at upper left, make diagonal stitches like regular Oriental except that there are 6 in each group instead of 4. The last stitch overlaps the zigzag edge of triangle of step 1 and touches at ends. Diagrams show compensation.

117

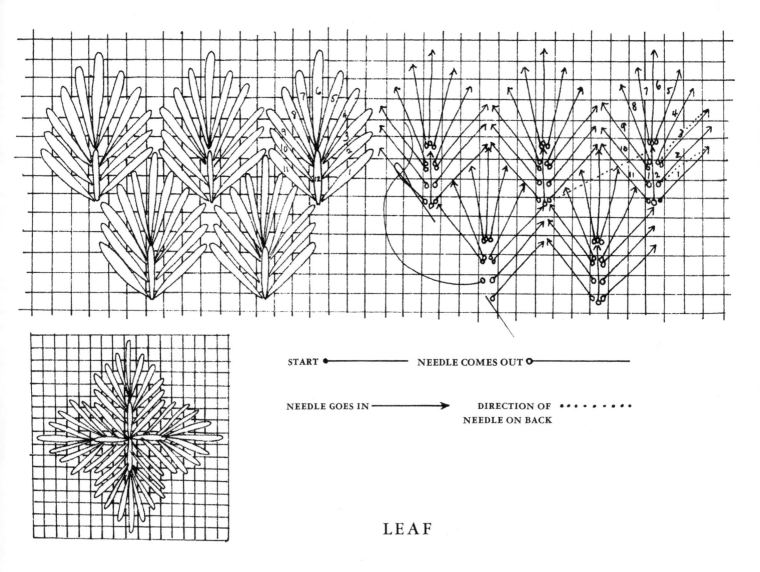

START ●————————— NEEDLE COMES OUT ○—————————

NEEDLE GOES IN ————————→   DIRECTION OF ● ● ● ● ● ● ● ●
                            NEEDLE ON BACK

LEAF

   Bring needle out where you want the base of the leaf to be. Insert needle up, right, over 3 intersections (1). Bring needle out 1 thread above beginning of first stitch. Make 2 more stitches directly above first stitch (2, 3). Bring needle out in the *same* hole as beginning of stitch 3, and insert it 1 intersection diagonally up, left of end of stitch 3 (4). Bring needle out 1 thread above beginnings of stitches 3 and 4, and insert it 1 intersection diagonally up, left of end of stitch 4 (5). Bring needle out in same hole as beginning of stitch 5 and insert it 5 threads straight up (6). This will be 1 intersection up, left of end of stitch 5, and forms the tip of the leaf.

   Match left side of leaf to right side, ending with yarn at base of leaf again. Make a vertical stitch over 3 threads to form midrib. This leaf pattern may be varied in proportions.

   Note: Although "plucking" (see preface) is not generally recommended, it is the easiest way to get the 12 stitches in their proper places.

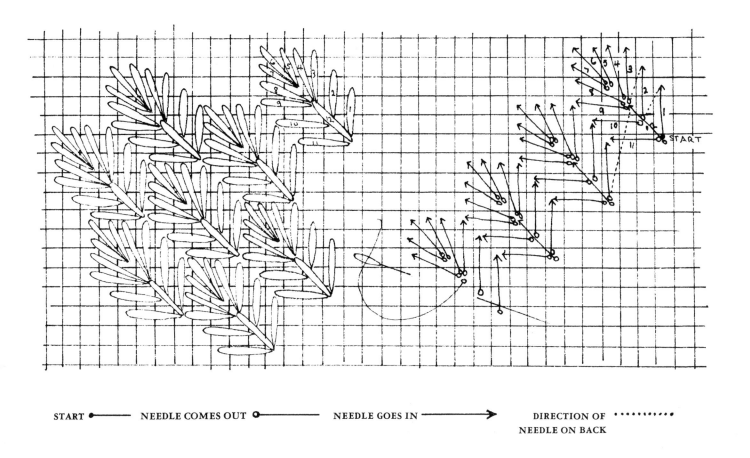

START •———— NEEDLE COMES OUT ○————— NEEDLE GOES IN ————→ DIRECTION OF • • • • • • • •
NEEDLE ON BACK

DIAGONAL LEAF

Begin with a vertical stitch over 3 threads (1). Make 2 more of these stitches diagonally up, left (2 and 3). The next stitch starts in the same hole as stitch 3. The needle is inserted 1 hole to the left of end of stitch 3 (4) and brought out 1 hole up, left, from beginnings of stitches 3 and 4 (5). The sixth stitch, the tip of the leaf, and the seventh begin in the same hole as the fifth. The sixth stitch covers 2 intersections. Match remaining stitches 8, 9, 10, and 11 to stitches 1, 2, 3, and 4 to complete other side of leaf. Make a midrib over 2 intersections (12).

The Diagonal Leaf pattern may be slanted in the opposite direction.

These units may be combined with regular Leaf (p. 118) to make an 8 petal flower form.

Note: Although "plucking" (see preface) is not generally recommended, it is the easiest way to get the 12 stitches in their proper places.

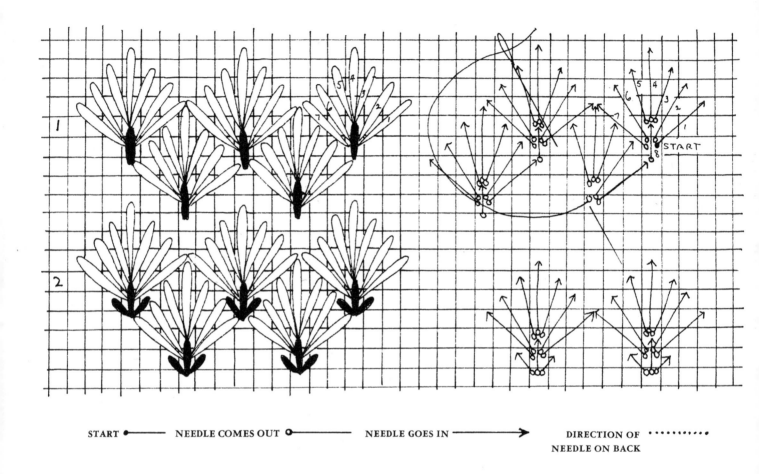

START ●——— NEEDLE COMES OUT ○——— NEEDLE GOES IN ———→ DIRECTION OF •••••••••
NEEDLE ON BACK

TIP OF LEAF

This stitch pattern covers a diagonal square with 4 holes on each side, counting corners twice. Begin 1 hole above base. First stitch covers 2 horizontal and 3 vertical threads, up, right. The second stitch starts in the same hole as the first stitch and needle is inserted 1 hole up, left, from end of first stitch. The third, fourth, and fifth stitches begin 1 hole above start of first and second stitches and use the top 3 holes of square. Stitches 6 and 7 are like 1 and 2 but in reverse.

Version 1 has 1 stitch over 2 threads at base, usually in a contrasting color.

Version 2 has the same center stitch as version 1, but with 2 diagonal stitches added over 1 intersection each.

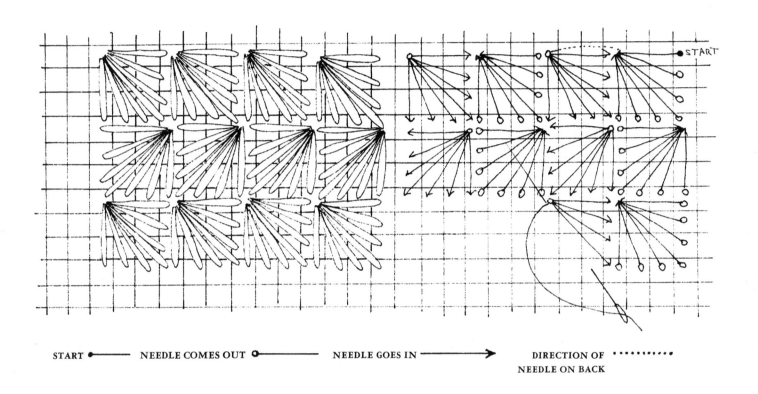

START ●————— NEEDLE COMES OUT ○————— NEEDLE GOES IN ——————→ DIRECTION OF ············
NEEDLE ON BACK

RAY

Ray stitch covers a 3-thread square, all 7 stitches radiating from 1 corner. In the first row, the upper left corner is used; in the second, the upper right.

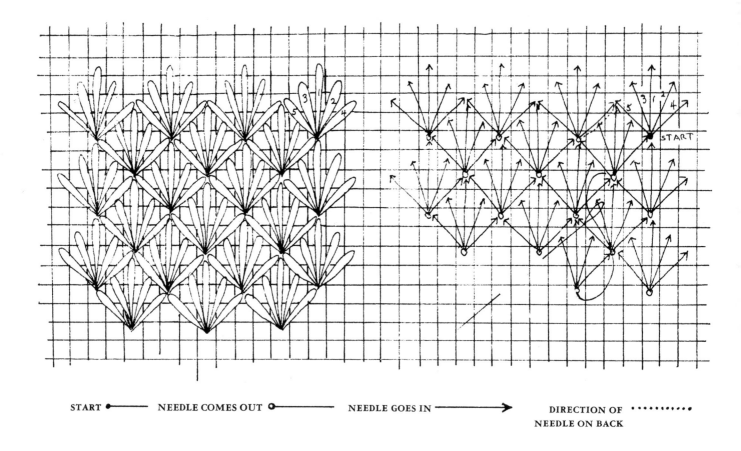

DIAMOND RAY

Five stitches, all originating at the base of a diagonal square, make this pattern. Because the stitches overlap at the base, it is best to work the center stitch first, then the two adjacent ones, and finally the side ones. Follow the numbers in the diagram.

122

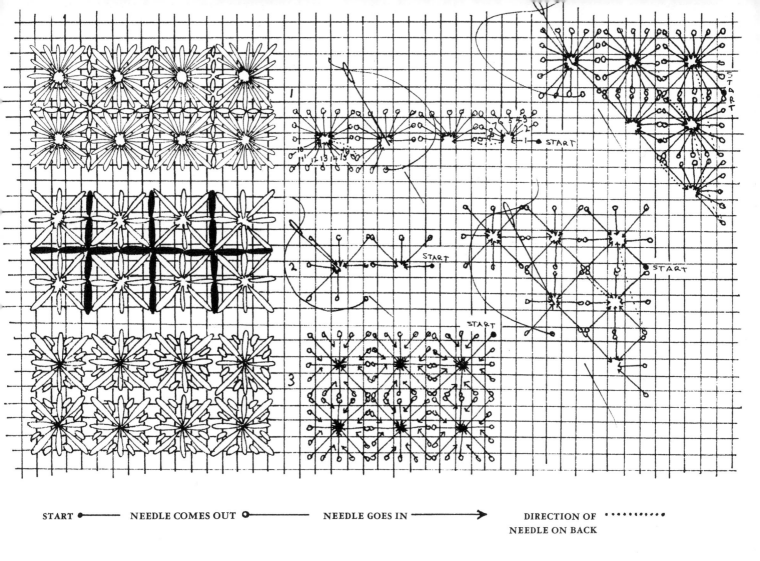

START ●————— NEEDLE COMES OUT ○————— NEEDLE GOES IN ————→ DIRECTION OF ●●●●●●●●●●
NEEDLE ON BACK

ALGERIAN EYE 1, 2, & 3
Star, Eye

1. This stitch pattern can be worked in either horizontal or diagonal rows. To cover a large area, either method can be used, but for a single row use the horizontal row method.

Horizontal row method. Work the top halves of the units, starting at the right, and finishing the units on the return journey. This is done to keep the tension on the stitches pulling in the proper direction. The needle must always come out at the edge of the unit and go down in the center hole. Pull yarn tight to form holes. Use fine yarn. Back stitches over 1 thread will be needed between units.

Diagonal row method. Start in upper right corner and work a complete unit. Then work top, right triangular halves of the units of the second row, finishing the lower left halves on return journey. Work succeeding rows in this manner.

2. This form of Algerian Eye is worked the same way, but only the vertical, horizontal, and diagonal stitches are used. Heavier yarn is used and little or no hole is made in the center. Back stitches over 2 threads are placed between units.

3. In this version the yarn is not pulled tight. Work complete units in horizontal rows.

Algerian Eye 2 and 3 are sometimes called Star stitch.

123

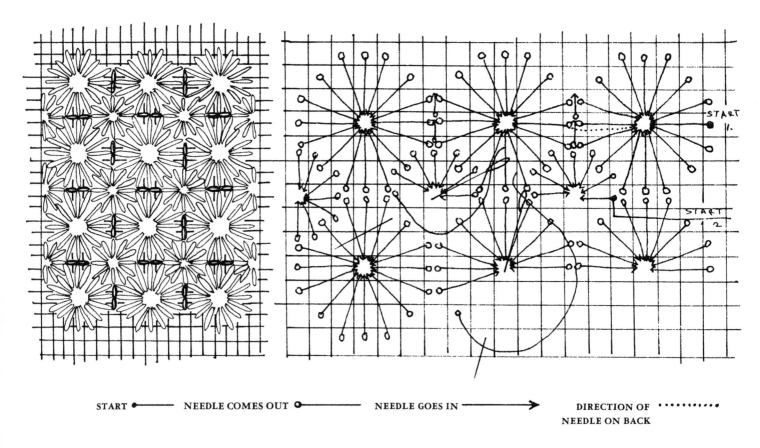

ALGERIAN EYE VARIATION 1

The large stitch pattern is similar to regular Algerian Eye (p. 123) except that the groups of 3 stitches on the sides cover 3 threads instead of 2. This creates circles or octagons instead of squares. When these stitch patterns are placed beside and below each other small diamond-shaped areas are left. These are covered with 12-stitch Eye patterns, 8 stitches of which encroach on main stitch patterns. Back stitches are needed between main stitch patterns.

Work main stitch patterns first, beginning at right and working the top halves of patterns. Then work lower halves on return journey from left to right. This keeps tension on stitches in proper direction to form symmetrical holes in the centers.

Use this same method to work small Eye patterns for step 2.

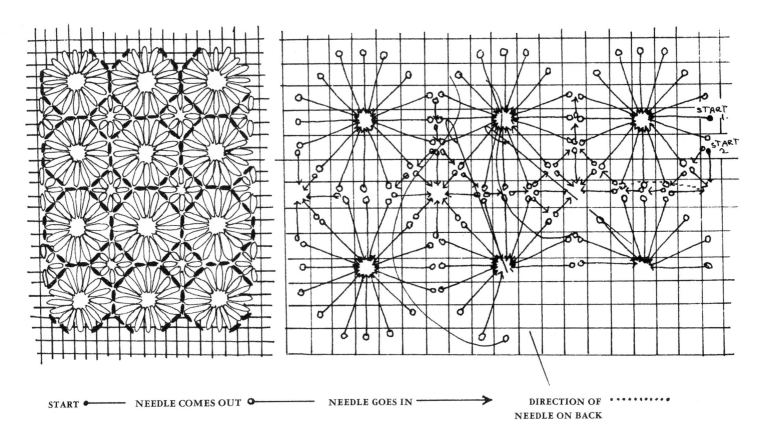

START ●——— NEEDLE COMES OUT ⟜——— NEEDLE GOES IN ⟶ DIRECTION OF ··········
NEEDLE ON BACK

ALGERIAN EYE VARIATION 2

   The main stitch pattern is the same as in variation 1, the 3 center stitches on the sides covering 3 threads instead of 2, as in regular Algerian Eye (p. 123). When these circular or octagonal stitch patterns are placed beside and below each other, diamond-shaped areas are left. These areas are covered by Eye patterns of 8 stitches each. Back stitches are needed around all sides of Eye stitch patterns.

   Work large units first, the top halves in first row, worked from right to left, then the lower halves to complete the units, worked from left to right. This keeps tension on stitches in proper direction to form symmetrical holes in centers. Use this same method to work smaller Eye patterns for step 2.

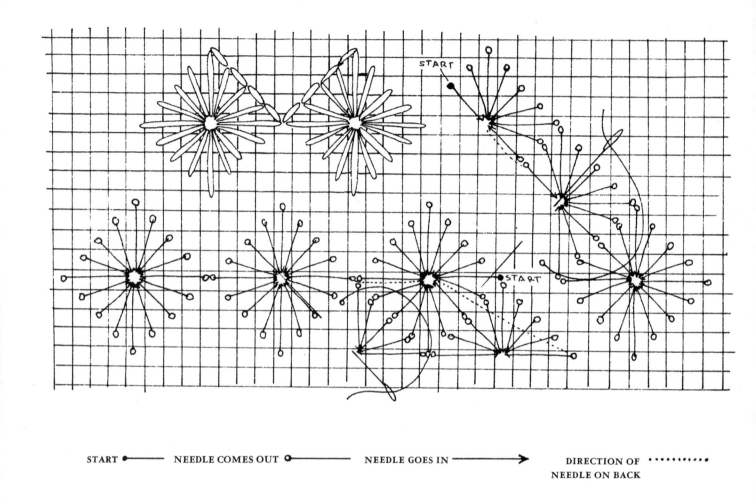

START ●—— NEEDLE COMES OUT ◦—— NEEDLE GOES IN ——→ DIRECTION OF ••••••••••
NEEDLE ON BACK

DIAMOND EYE

For straight rows, starting at the right, work the top triangular halves of the diamonds and complete lower halves on return journey.

For diagonal rows, work rectangular halves, upper right sides, and complete on return journey.

The needle comes out at perimeter and is inserted in center hole. Pull yarn tight. The diamonds are worked half at a time to keep the tension on the stitches in the proper direction. Use medium weight yarn, not fine. The hole in the center will not be very large, but if fine yarn is used, it will not cover the canvas at outer edges of units. Back stitches are needed between units to cover exposed canvas intersections.

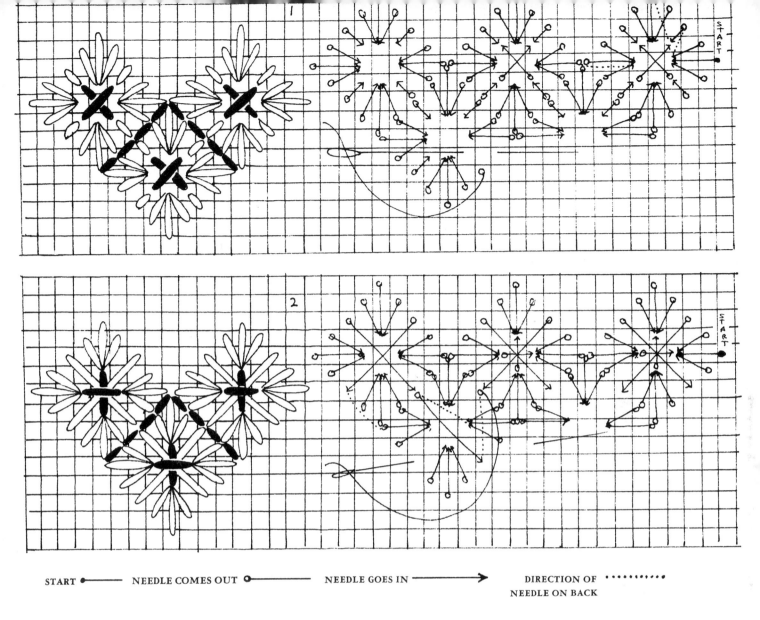

DIAMOND EYE VARIATIONS 1 & 2

Diamond Eye Variation 1. Starting at the right make the top halves of the stitch patterns across the row. Needle comes up at the edge and goes down near the center. Complete bottom halves of stitch patterns on return journey. The stitch pattern covers a diagonal square 5 holes to a side, counting corners twice. The 3 corner stitches use a common hole 3 threads in from corner. Diagonal stitches over 1 intersection each are worked between them. This leaves a 4-thread square in the center which is covered by a diagonal cross stitch.

Diamond Eye Variation 2. The same 3 corner stitches are used, but instead of the 4 short stitches between them, a large diagonal cross stitch is placed completely across unit. Then a straight cross is placed over the center of this large cross. Back stitches over 1 intersection each may be placed between units.

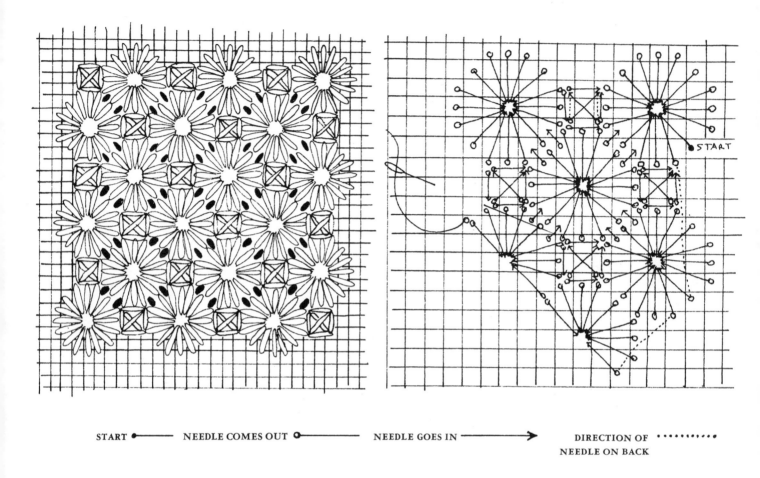

START ●————— NEEDLE COMES OUT ○————— NEEDLE GOES IN ————————▶ DIRECTION OF ● ● ● ● ● ● ● ● ●
NEEDLE ON BACK

DIAMOND EYE VARIATION 3

This is a combination of modified Diamond Eye (p. 126), Italian Cross (p. 29), and Tent stitches.

Work regular Diamond Eye except make the corner stitches over 3 threads instead of 4, forming an octagon. Work in diagonal rows, the upper right half of units on first journey, and completing lower left half on return journey. Pull yarn tight. This leaves 4-thread squares between units. Cover these squares with small Italian Crosses. Then with fine yarn, work Tent stitch between units of Diamond Eye with stitches parallel to those of Diamond Eye. It will be a little difficult to find the holes for the Tent stitches because of the distortion of the canvas threads caused by the Diamond Eye stitches. Two or three colors make an effective design.

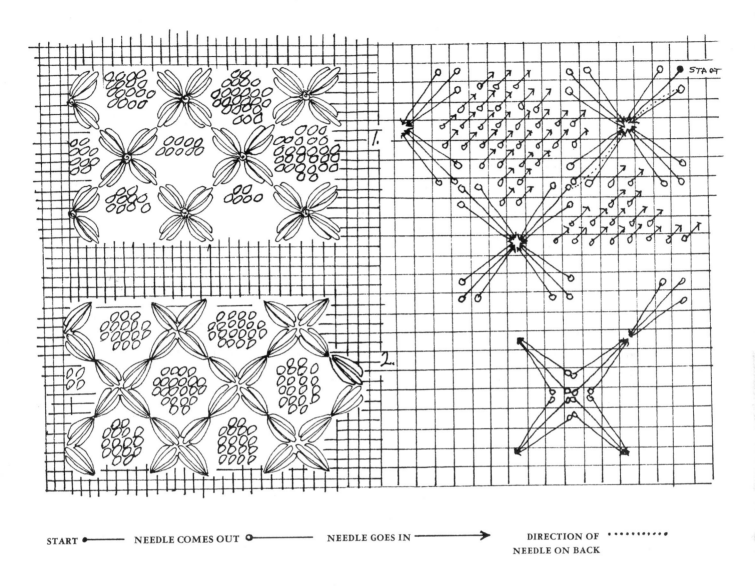

START ●━━━ NEEDLE COMES OUT ○━━━ NEEDLE GOES IN ━━━━▶ DIRECTION OF ···········
NEEDLE ON BACK

DIAMOND EYE VARIATIONS WITH TENT

1. Starting at upper right, make a diagonal stitch over 3 intersections down, left. Bring needle out 1 hole to left of start. Insert needle in same hole as first stitch and bring it out 1 hole below start. Insert needle in center hole and bring it out 3 intersections up, left. Make a second group of 3 stitches, using same center hole. Now make 2 more groups opposite to these groups, bringing needle out at lower end of diagonal stitch in lower left group. Repeat these groups diagonally across area. Other rows are arranged so that tips of diagonal stitches touch. If you wish, French Knots (p. 150) can be placed in the centers.

Cover the rest of the area with Diagonal Tent stitch (p. 90) working as close to the Eye stitch forms as is necessary to cover the canvas.

2. Version 2 is essentially the same except the other ends of the 3 stitch forms are brought together.

129

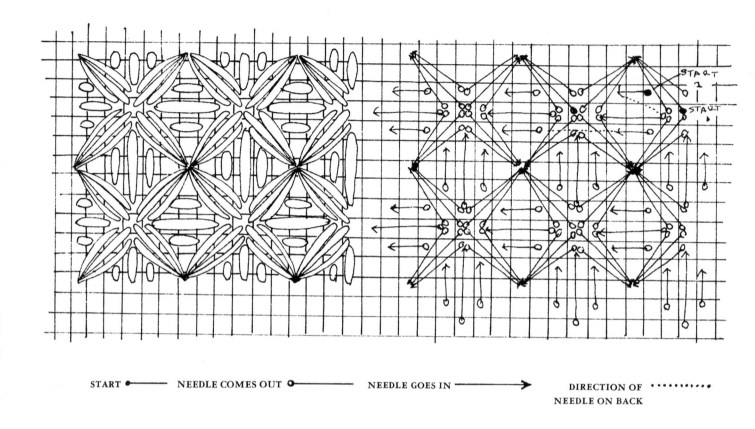

START •———— NEEDLE COMES OUT •————— NEEDLE GOES IN ————→ DIRECTION OF •••••••••
NEEDLE ON BACK

EYE VARIATION WITH HUNGARIAN

Make a diagonal stitch up, left, over 3 intersections. Bring the needle out 1 hole above start and insert it in the same hole as stitch 1 (2). Bring the needle out 1 hole to left of start and insert it in same hole as stitch 1 (3). Bring the needle out 3 intersections down, left, and insert it in same hole as stitch 1 (4). Now make 2 more stitches starting above and to the right of start of stitch 4 (5, 6), and bring the needle out at start of stitch 4. Repeat these 6 stitches across horizontal row, bringing the needle out at start of last diagonal stitch. Make the second row from left to right with the common hole down instead of up. Repeat rows 1 and 2 over area.

Fill in with Hungarian stitch units (p. 8), the long stitches across the center of the spaces. In the first row the units are horizontal and in the second row they are vertical.

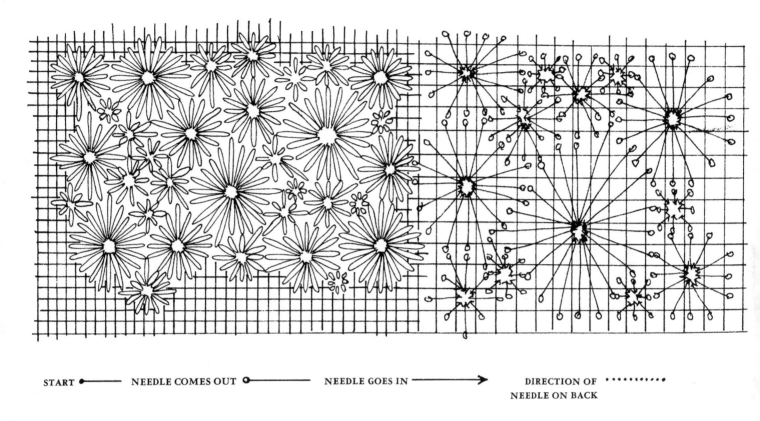

START ●———— NEEDLE COMES OUT ⊙———— NEEDLE GOES IN ————→ DIRECTION OF ···········• NEEDLE ON BACK

HIT-A-MISS EYE

    Fit Eye stitches together, "hit-a-miss," varying the size of units. The units are more or less round and will not fit together smoothly. Little units can be worked in between large ones, even if there are as few as 2 threads each way. Exposed threads and intersections are covered with back stitches, both straight and diagonal.

131

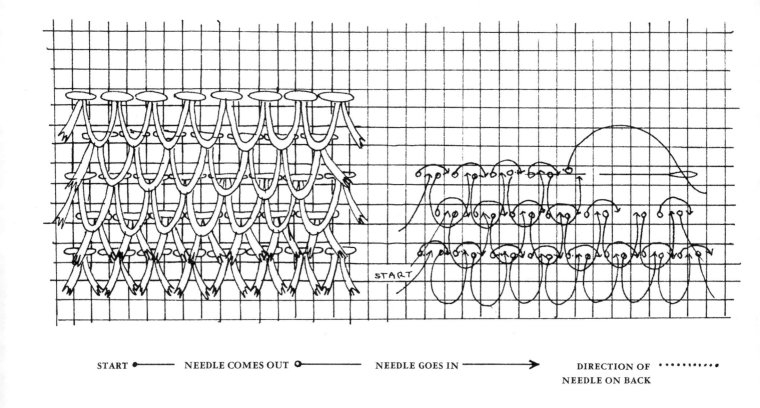

START ●————— NEEDLE COMES OUT ○————— NEEDLE GOES IN ————————➤ DIRECTION OF ·············
                                                                 NEEDLE ON BACK

TURKEY KNOT*
Tufting

Begin this stitch pattern from the front of the canvas and work from the bottom up. Starting at bottom, left of area to be covered, and, holding the loose end with your left thumb, put the needle under 1 vertical thread of the canvas from right to left. With working strand held above work area, put the needle under next vertical thread to the right, again from right to left, bringing it out in same hole as start of first stitch. Put point of needle through yarn of first stitch. This serves to keep stitches from pulling out after they are cut. Pull yarn down toward you firmly. Hold a loop of yarn with your thumb and repeat, using the next pair of vertical threads. Repeat across row. Cut yarn of working strand and begin again at the left 2 threads up and 1 thread to the right so rows are staggered. The loops may be cut to form tufting. Use yarn that fluffs well when cut. The diagram doesn't do justice to the way this stitch pattern looks. If fluffy yarn is used, you will get a mixed mound of cut ends with no stitches showing. Make loops longer than those in the diagram. The cut ends can be trimmed fairly short (¼ inch). Interesting effects can be obtained by varying the depth of the nap.

This stitch pattern is effective when shaded. It is good for fringe, rugs, or to simulate fur.

* Left-handed people reverse "left" and "right."

132

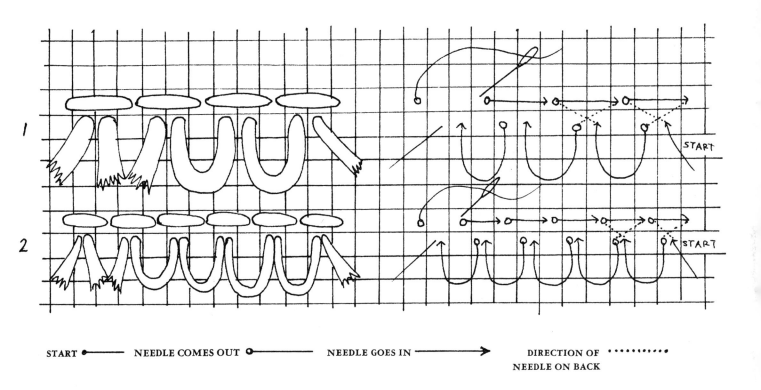

START ●——— NEEDLE COMES OUT ⦵——— NEEDLE GOES IN ————→ DIRECTION OF ·········
NEEDLE ON BACK

KNOTTED TUFTING*

1. Begin all rows at the right with the yarn on the front of the canvas, not brought through from the back, and also make first row at the bottom of the area you wish to cover. Pass needle under 1 horizontal and 2 vertical threads, up, left. Insert needle 3 threads to right and bring it out 1 horizontal and 2 vertical threads, down, left (the hole to the left of your starting point). Pull down drawing stitch tight. Hold a loop of yarn with your left thumb (longer than in diagram) and repeat these 2 stitches across row. At end of row cut yarn and begin again at the right. Move up 2 threads and over 1 thread to left or right so stitch patterns will not be directly above each other.

2. The smaller version is similar to Tufting or Turkey Knot except that the top stitch is reversed, forming a "V" shape on the back. An added advantage is that the stitches will not slide out of place on the canvas. The procedure is the same as in version 1 except that the needle passes under 1 intersection, the top stitch covers 2 threads, and there is no thread between loops.

This stitch is good for fringe, rugs, or to simulate fur.

* Left-handed people reverse "left" and "right."

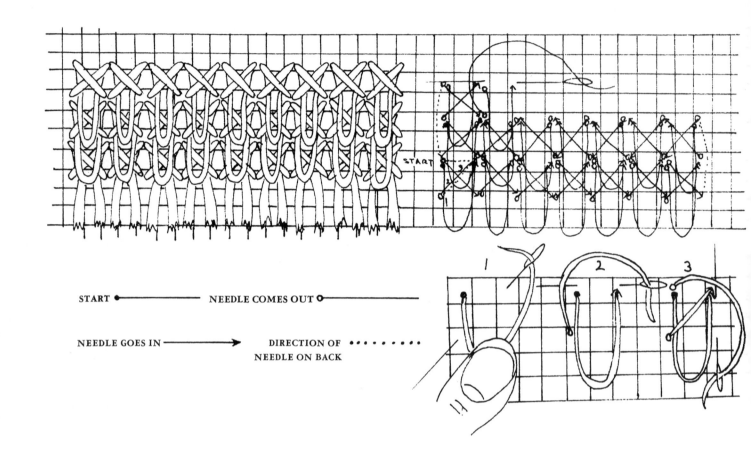

START ●————————— NEEDLE COMES OUT ○—————————

NEEDLE GOES IN ————————→   DIRECTION OF • • • • • • • •
                                NEEDLE ON BACK

ASTRAKHAN VELVET*
Velvet

Make a loop (1) and cover the top of it with a 2 intersection Cross stitch (2, 3). This stitch pattern starts at bottom left of area to be covered. Hold loop with left thumb while making Cross stitch (p. 25). The stitches of the second row are directly above those of the first row. This pattern forms a very secure loop. Use heavy yarn that fluffs well when cut. This pattern is good for fringe, rugs, or to simulate fur. If heavy yarn is used, 1 canvas thread may be left between rows. The diagram at left doesn't do justice to the way this stitch pattern looks. If fluffy yarn is used you will get a mixed mound of fluffy cut ends with no stitches showing. Make loops longer than those in diagram. The cut ends can be trimmed fairly short (¼ inch) if desired. Interesting effects can be obtained by varying the depth of the nap. The stitch pattern is very effective when shaded.

This pattern is ideal to finish pillows, as the crosses are worked over the seam, covering it completely.

---

* Left-handed people reverse "left" and "right."

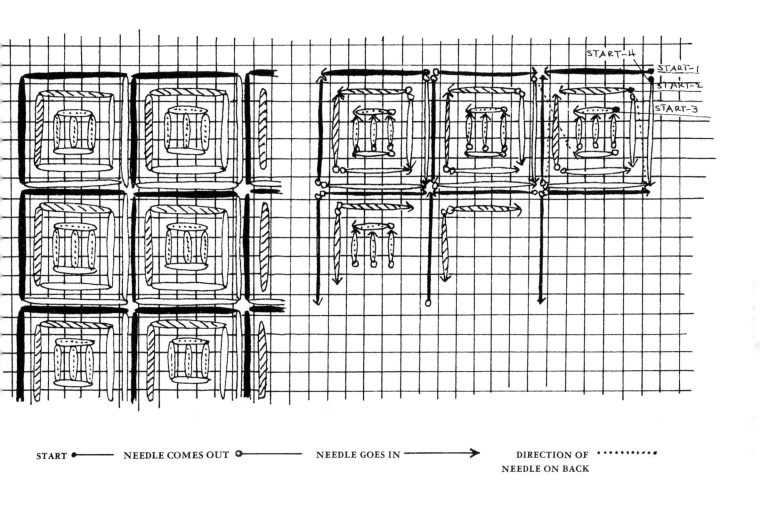

START ●━━━━ NEEDLE COMES OUT ○━━━━ NEEDLE GOES IN ━━━━▶ DIRECTION OF ••••••••••
NEEDLE ON BACK

SHADOW BOX

This is worked in at least 3 shades of 1 color. The diagram shows 4. The long outside stitches cover 6 threads, the second set 4, and the inside is made up of 3 vertical stitches and 2 horizontal ones. The longest stitches of 1 box use the same holes as longest stitches of adjacent boxes. This crowds the yarn slightly causing slight ridges. Work the darkest color first, then the second and so on to the lightest.

This stitch pattern can be worked in 1 color. To do so work 1 unit at a time.

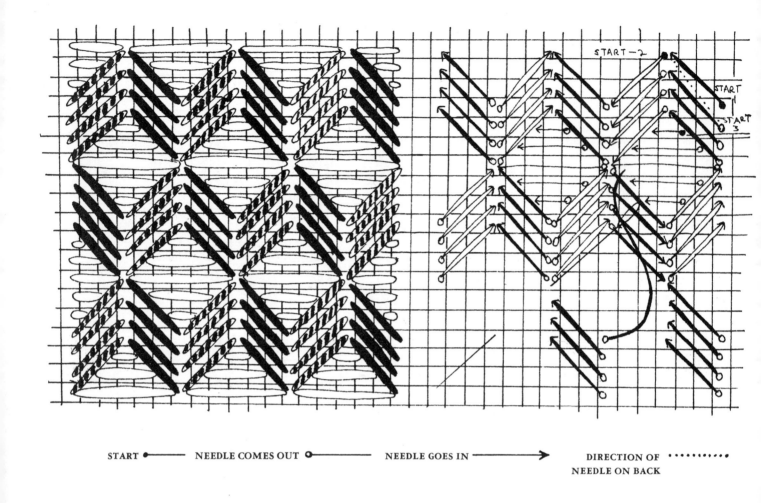

START ●————— NEEDLE COMES OUT ○————— NEEDLE GOES IN ————→ DIRECTION OF ••••••••••
NEEDLE ON BACK

STACKED CUBES

The name for this stitch pattern comes from the illusion created by the natural shading of the stitches. It can be worked in 3 shades of 1 color or all in 1 shade.

Step 1. At right side of area work 4 diagonal stitches, one below the other, each covering 3 intersections. Then, 3 threads to left, work 4 more diagonal stitches slanting in the same direction at the same height as first group. Continue across row in this manner. Leave the end of working strand loose at end of first row.

Step 2. Work groups of 4 diagonal stitches in a lighter shade between groups of stitches of step 1, pointing in the opposite direction, and connecting with stitches of step 1. Continue across row in this manner. In the second row the tops of stitches meet the bottoms of stitches of row 1, leaving a diagonal square unworked. All stitches pointing in one direction are worked in the same shade. The groups will not be under each other. It is best to carry both steps along together so as to be sure to place the stitches properly.

Step 3. In lightest shade, work groups of horizontal stitches over squares. The stitches cover 2, 4, 6, 4, 2 vertical threads.

136

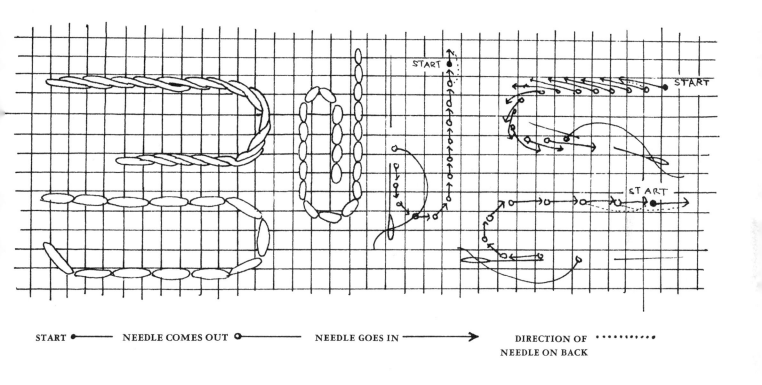

START •———— NEEDLE COMES OUT o———— NEEDLE GOES IN ————→ DIRECTION OF • • • • • • • • • •
NEEDLE ON BACK

OUTLINE*   BACK*
Cable

Outline (Cable).   Bring needle out at the left end of row. Carry yarn over 3 threads. Insert needle and bring it out 2 threads to the left, and either above or below first stitch. Continue across row in this manner, bringing needle out either above or below previous stitch, whichever you chose for first stitch. By varying the direction and length of the stitches, this stitch pattern can be worked around curves. The needle points in direction opposite to that of the row.

Back Stitch.   Starting at right bring needle out 1 or 2 threads to the left of end of line to be worked. Insert needle at end of the line and bring it out 2 or 4 threads to the left. Insert needle at end of first stitch and repeat. This stitch pattern gives the finest outline and is often used between units of other stitch patterns where canvas threads may show. It is good for separating colors that are too much alike. It can be worked diagonally over 1 or 2 intersections. The needle points in the direction of the row.

* Left-handed people reverse "left" and "right."

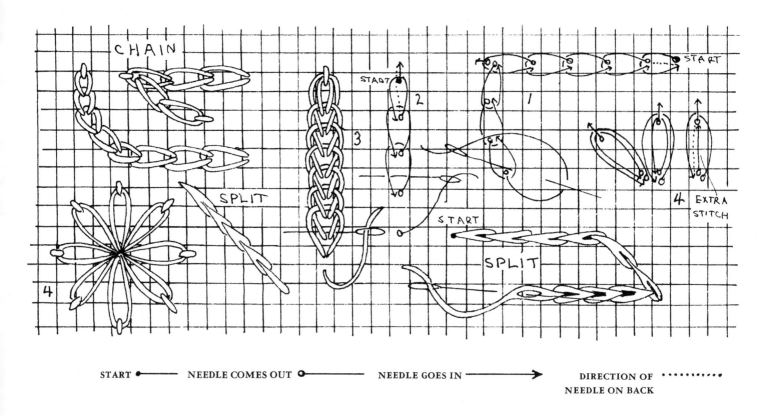

START •————— NEEDLE COMES OUT ○————— NEEDLE GOES IN ————————▶ DIRECTION OF • • • • • • • • • •
NEEDLE ON BACK

CHAIN 1, 2, 3 & 4   SPLIT*

1. Chain 1.   Bring needle out from back and put it in in the same hole, leaving a loop. Bring needle out 2 threads to left and pass it through the loop of first stitch. Pull to make loop smaller but not too snug. Insert needle through first loop and hole in canvas where needle came out and bring it out 2 threads to the left. Repeat. When working Chain stitch around a sharp angle, put a small fastening stitch at end of corner loop to hold it in place.

2. Chain 2 (Reverse).   Make a small stitch over 1 horizontal thread at top. Bring needle out 2 threads down. Pass the needle through small stitch but not under canvas threads. Insert needle in same hole as start of stitch and bring it out 2 threads down. Now pass the needle under both sides of loop of second stitch. Insert needle into same hole as start of stitch and repeat.

3. Chain 3 or *Hungarian Braided Chain.*   This is a form of Reverse Chain. Start with fastening stitch. First Chain stitch covers 2 threads. The second stitch covers 1 or 2 threads and uses the fastening stitch too. When making third and following stitches pass needle over both legs of previous stitch, and under both legs of stitch before that. Any form of Chain stitch can be worked straight, diagonally, or around curves. Slight variations in the length of the stitches will not show.

4. Chain 4 or *Single or Double Detached Chain* (Lazy Daisy).   These units make effective flower petals, or parts of geometric designs. If canvas shows in center of single unit, a straight stitch may be added to cover it. Both forms may be worked straight, diagonally, or slanting. They may vary greatly in size, and can be worked on top of other patterns.

Split.   This stitch pattern is similar to the Outline (Cable) stitch (p. 137), except that instead of bringing the needle out beside previous stitch, the needle is passed through the stitch, splitting the yarn. This stitch pattern is very useful for outlining, as it takes up very little space and is compact. It can be worked around curves and angles. It looks like a fine Chain stitch. The length of the stitch can vary and won't show.

* Left-handed people reverse "left" and "right."

138

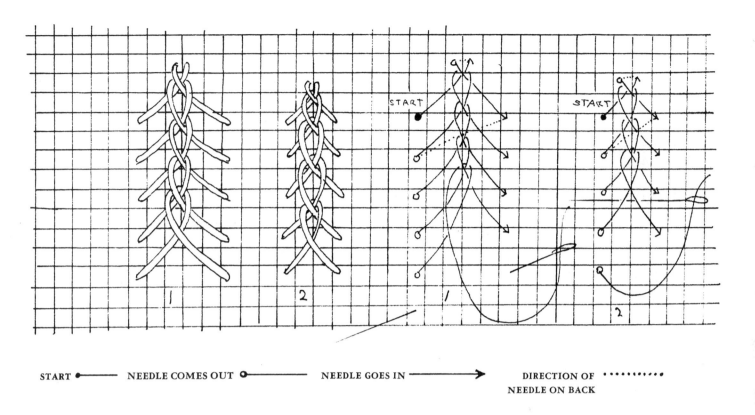

START ●——— NEEDLE COMES OUT ⊶——— NEEDLE GOES IN ——→ DIRECTION OF ●●●●●●●●●●
NEEDLE ON BACK

VAN DYKE*

1. Bring needle out 5 vertical threads to the left and 3 horizontal threads down in the area to be covered. Insert needle 3 intersections up, right. Bring it out 1 thread to the left and insert it 3 intersections down, right. Bring it out 2 threads below start of first stitch. In the next stitch, instead of putting the needle under 1 thread, pass it under just the 2 crossed stitches of first unit, but don't penetrate the canvas. Then insert needle 2 threads below end of second stitch of first unit. Continue in a vertical row in this manner. A ridge is formed down the middle with rays extending to the sides.

2. Shorter side extensions can be obtained by allowing 3 threads between ends of stitches instead of 5. The first 2 stitches cover 2 intersections instead of 3.

By itself this stitch pattern does not cover the canvas so it is not used to cover an area. It is effective when used as an outline with the side parts extending over other stitches. It also can be used with other stitch patterns which have long side stitches, such as Plaited (p. 52), Plaited Gobelin (p. 53), Loop (p. 144), Buttonhole (p. 143), etc. It can be worked diagonally.

* Left-handed people reverse "left" and "right."

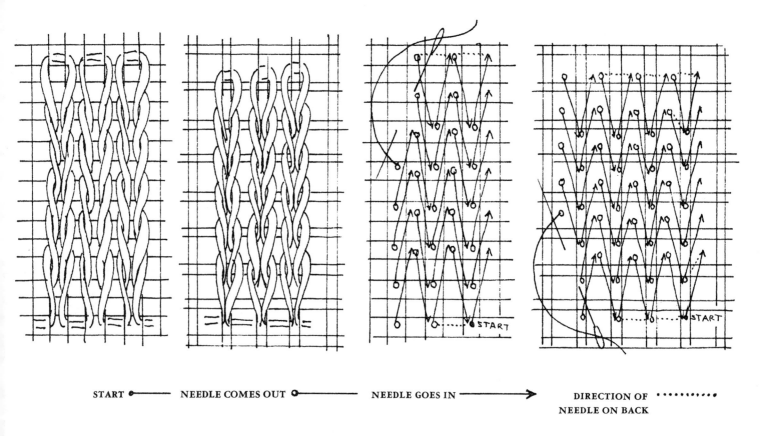

START ●━━━━━→ NEEDLE COMES OUT ○━━━━━ NEEDLE GOES IN ━━━━━━━→ DIRECTION OF ••••••••••
NEEDLE ON BACK

KNITTING 3*

Most books advise working this stitch pattern on double mesh canvas, but it is equally effective on single mesh. Work in vertical rows.

Ascending row—On double mesh canvas bring needle out between close-placed vertical threads in space between groups of 2 horizontal threads. From here on directions pertain to both kinds of canvas. Make a slanting stitch over 4 horizontal and 1 vertical threads, up, right. Bring needle out 1 thread to left and 2 threads down. Repeat to top of row. Now pass the needle under 2 threads to the left and reverse procedure for descending row. Again pass the needle under 2 threads to the left and start another ascending row. The result looks much like rows of Chain stitch or stockinette stitch in knitting.

* Left-handed people reverse "left" and "right."

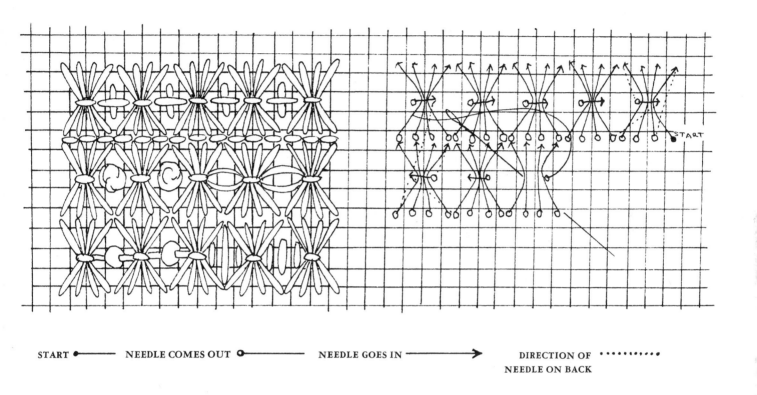

START ●———— NEEDLE COMES OUT ○————— NEEDLE GOES IN ————————▶ DIRECTION OF •••••••••
NEEDLE ON BACK

SHELL*
Sheaf

Work 4 vertical stitches over 4 threads. Then by pushing aside the last stitch toward the right, bring the needle out 2 threads down and 1 thread to the right. Push the first stitch out of the way to the left, and insert the needle 1 hole to right of where it came out. Bring needle out in the same hole as used by the bottom of stitch 4 of first group, drawing yarn snug to form sheaf. Repeat.

This stitch pattern is usually used in single rows for its decorative quality. If more than one row is used to cover an area, back stitches will be needed between rows to cover canvas.

The spaces left between sheafs can be filled in many ways, as indicated in the left diagram. You can use Straight Crosses, a running horizontal strand through the tie stitches, beads threaded on horizontal stitches, large French Knots (p. 150), or 3 vertical stitches, either all the same size or with the center one long, to name but a few.

* Left-handed people reverse "left" and "right."

141

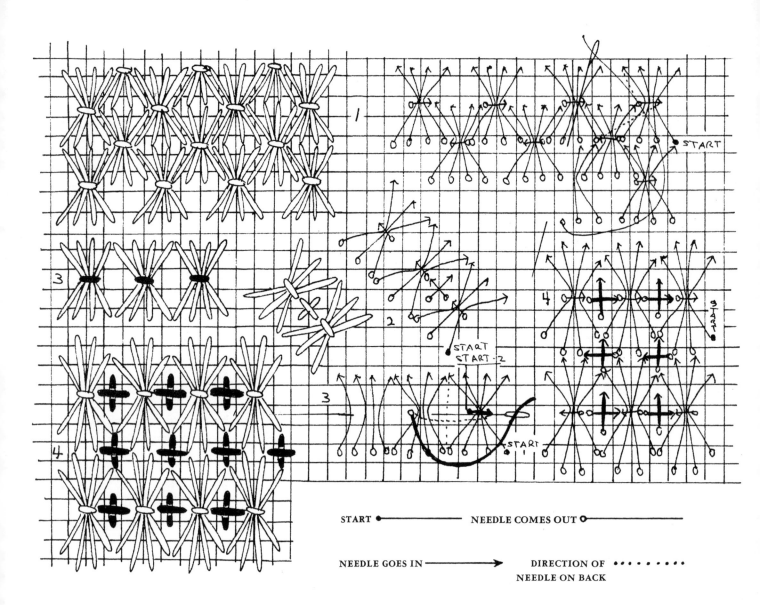

SHELL VARIATIONS 1, 2, 3, & 4*
Sheaf Variations

1. This stitch pattern is worked like regular Shell or Sheaf except that 1 vertical thread is left between stitch clusters. The second row fits halfway up between the sheafs of first row. The tie stitch uses the vertical thread left between the units of the first row. The half sheaves for compensation are at the top of the left diagram.

2. Work the diagonal version over 3 intersections, 3 stitches to a sheaf. The tie stitch is made over the middle intersection between the ends of the middle stitch of the cluster.

3. It is possible to make the tie stitch of regular Shell or Sheaf of a contrasting color. To do this carry both colors along as you work.

4. In this version the center 2 stitches of each unit cover 6 threads instead of 4. To cover an area combine this version with Straight Cross between units and between rows.

* Left-handed people reverse "left" and "right."

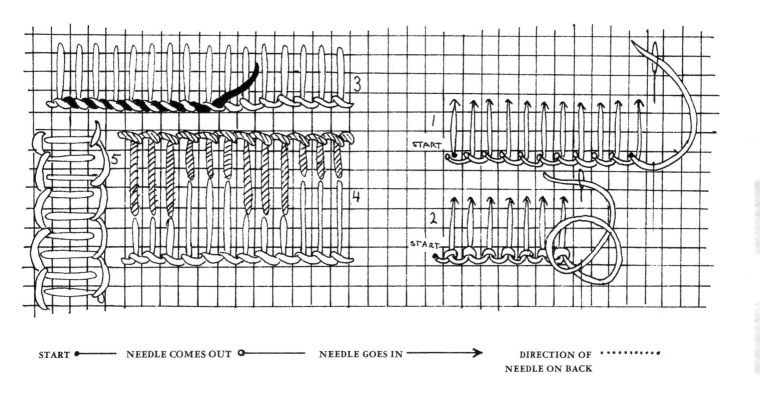

START ●————— NEEDLE COMES OUT ○————— NEEDLE GOES IN ————————▶ DIRECTION OF • • • • • • • • • • •
NEEDLE ON BACK

BUTTONHOLE & BUTTONHOLE VARIATIONS

Diagram 1 shows a simple Buttonhole stitch. Vertical stitches are made over 3 or more horizontal threads, using every hole with needle pointing down. The point of the needle passes over yarn of stitch, bending it in the form of a J. This forms a cablelike edge at bottom of stitches. It is necessary to make a straight stitch at beginning of row to fill the space. Rows begin at left.

Diagram 2 is called Tailor's Buttonhole stitch. This is produced the same way except that an extra loop is made, like a French Knot, drawn snug, and then the needle is pulled through. This forms a knotted edge.

Diagram 3 shows a simple Buttonhole with a contrasting color worked through the looped edge without penetrating the canvas.

Diagrams 4 and 5 are two more variations of simple Buttonhole. There are many more variations possible. Buttonhole can also be combined with other stitch patterns or worked on top of other stitchery.

143

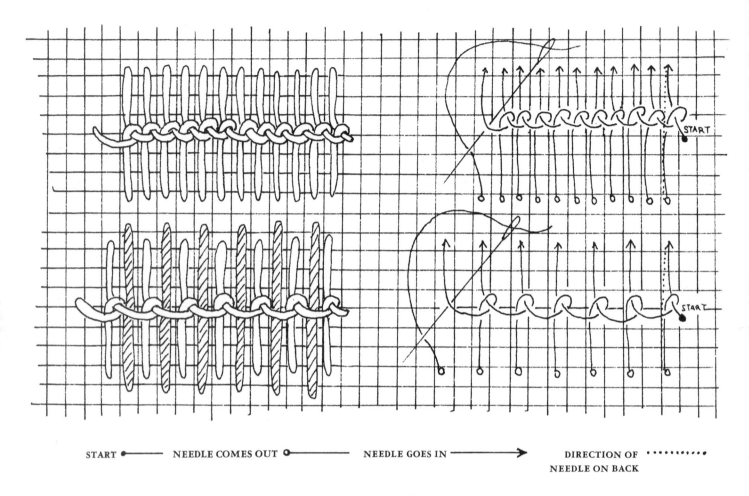

START ●————— NEEDLE COMES OUT ○————— NEEDLE GOES IN ————▶ DIRECTION OF ●●●●●●●●●●●
                                                          NEEDLE ON BACK

LOOP*

Make a stitch over 4 horizontal and 1 vertical threads, bringing the needle out 7 threads directly below end of first stitch. Keep excess yarn to left and pass needle under first stitch from right to left and over excess yarn. Then insert needle at top again 1 thread to the left of end of first stitch. Continue in this manner using every hole. A pleasing effect is produced by using every other hole and filling in the spaces with straight stitches in a contrasting color.

* Left-handed people reverse "left" and "right."

144

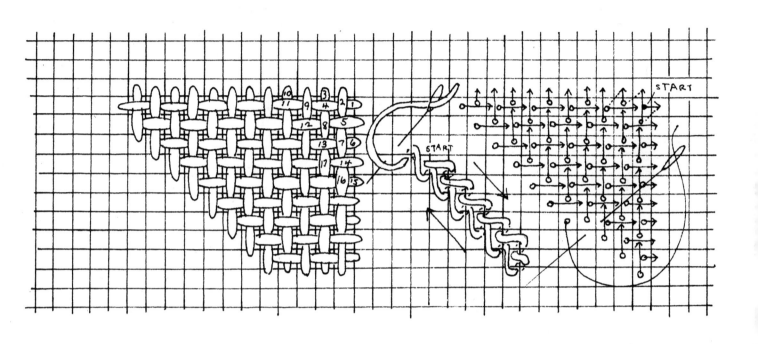

START ●——— NEEDLE COMES OUT ○——— NEEDLE GOES IN ———→ DIRECTION OF •••••••••
NEEDLE ON BACK

BASKET WEAVE*
Back Side of Diagonal Tent

This stitch pattern is formed by making Diagonal Tent stitches (p. 90) on the back of the canvas and Basket Weave on the front. The yarn is carried over 2 horizontal threads in the descending row, and over 2 vertical threads in the ascending row. There is a short stitch over 1 thread at the end of each row. The needle is passed under 1 intersection from upper right to lower left for *all* stitches. This produces the Diagonal Tent stitch on the back of the canvas.

* Left-handed people turn diagram halfway around (top at bottom) and start in lower left corner.

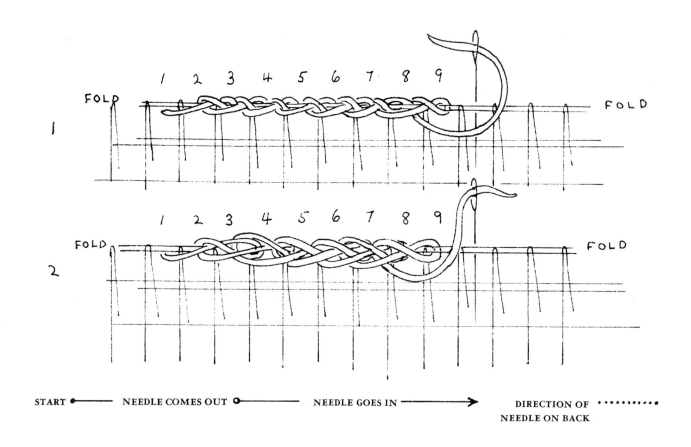

START ●——— NEEDLE COMES OUT ○——— NEEDLE GOES IN ——————→ DIRECTION OF ••••••••••
NEEDLE ON BACK

BINDING STITCH

The Binding stitch can be used to make a strong decorative edge on a rug, mat, coaster, etc. It can also be used as a seam to join two finished pieces; for example, halves of eyeglass case. It covers well and goes around corners readily.

The diagrams do not show the 3-dimensional quality. The needle is held in a horizontal position, pointing straight toward you, and the folded canvas is held vertically. The needle passes from back to front through folded edge for all stitches.

1. Small size. Bring the needle out from inside the fold at 1. Pass the needle through 2 holes on the fold at 3. Back to 2, then to 4, back to 3, then to 5, etc. The sequence is 1–3, 2–4, 3–5, 4–6, 5–7, etc.

2. Large size. The procedure is the same as for the small size, but the stitches are longer. The sequence is 1–4, 2–5, 3–6, 4–7, 5–8, etc.

146

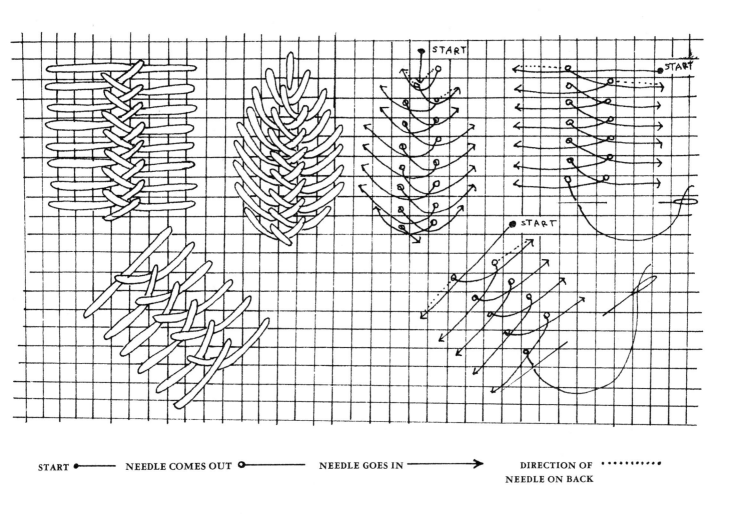

START ●——— NEEDLE COMES OUT ○————— NEEDLE GOES IN ——————→ DIRECTION OF •••••••••
NEEDLE ON BACK

CRETAN*

This stitch pattern is really a closed Feather stitch. It can be worked in vertical or diagonal rows. A long stitch at the top makes a neat edge. By starting with a vertical stitch over 2 threads and varying the length of the stitches, a leaf form is made. Heavy yarn is needed for the diagonal form. This forms a pattern that looks like a braid down the middle.

* Left-handed people reverse "left" and "right."

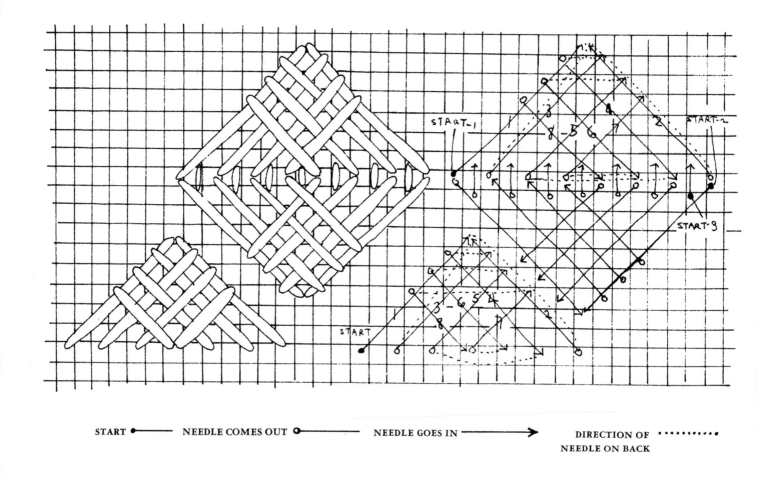

START ●————— NEEDLE COMES OUT ○————— NEEDLE GOES IN ————————▶ DIRECTION OF ••••••••••
NEEDLE ON BACK

SPRAT'S HEAD*

Start with 2 long diagonal stitches at right angles to each other. Make them the same length, the length depending on the size you wish your stitch pattern to be (7, 8, 9 intersections). These stitches use a common hole at the top. The needle is inserted in the top hole to finish the second stitch. Bring needle out 2 threads to the right of bottom of stitch 1. Insert the needle 1 intersection down, right from top ends of first 2 stitches (3), and bring it out 1 intersection down, left from top ends of original stitches. These stitches pass over the original 2 stitches. Insert the needle 2 threads to the left of the bottom of stitch 2 (4). Bring it out 2 threads to right of bottom end of stitch 3. Insert needle 1 intersection down, right from end of stitch 3. Bring needle out 1 intersection down, left from top of stitch 4. Continue in this manner until bottoms of stitches use a common hole or are 2 threads apart.

A second Sprat's Head placed beneath the first forms a square. Vertical stitches are needed between units to cover canvas.

* Left-handed people reverse "left" and "right."

148

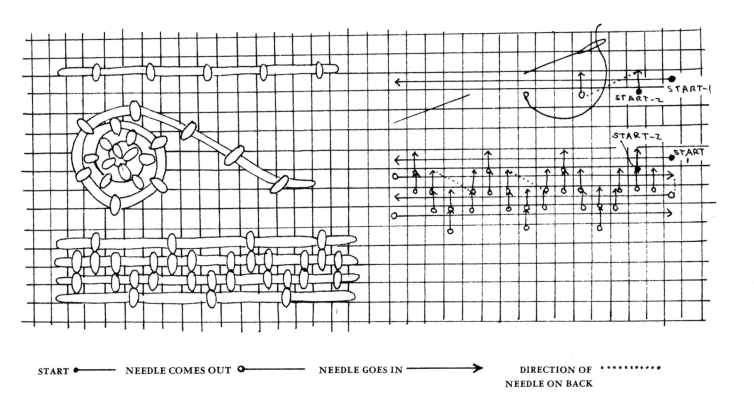

START ●——— **NEEDLE COMES OUT** ⦵——— **NEEDLE GOES IN** ——————▶ **DIRECTION OF** • • • • • • • • • •
NEEDLE ON BACK

COUCHING*

Simple Couching is a series of short stitches made over a long strand to fasten it to a surface. In canvas work this is often done over other stitching when irregular shapes are required. The top diagram shows the simplest form. Because the base strand lies on top of the canvas except at its ends, unmanageable material that cannot be drawn through the canvas can be used.

By varying the distance between stitches of the couching strand, interesting effects can be obtained.

Several strands can be couched at once with longer stitches.

Other stitch patterns can be used for couching (see Herringbone Couching, p. 49). Couching has many, many possible variations. It can be worked on top of other stitchery.

---

* Left-handed people reverse "left" and "right."

149

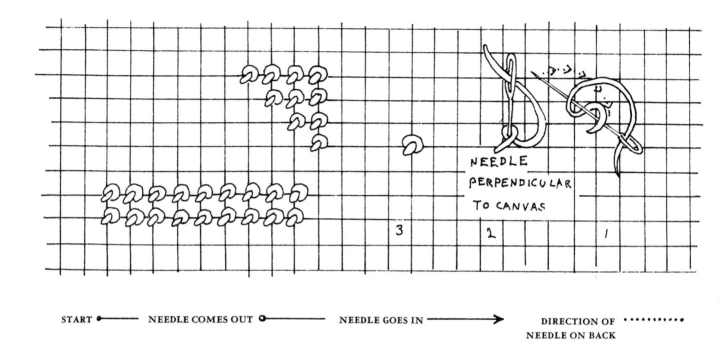

NEEDLE
PERPENDICULAR
TO CANVAS

3   2   I

START ●——— NEEDLE COMES OUT ○——— NEEDLE GOES IN ————➤ DIRECTION OF ●●●●●●●●●●
                                                        NEEDLE ON BACK

FRENCH KNOTS*

   Bring yarn out from back as for Tent stitch. Holding eye of needle in right hand, wind yarn around needle one or two times toward point. Insert needle into hole diagonally up, right. Holding needle at right angles to canvas, draw yarn tight with left hand. Push needle through and draw yarn snug on back of piece. This forms a French Knot on the top of a regular Tent stitch.
   Massed tightly together, French Knots produce a high nubby surface.
   Use finer yarn than for Tent stitch. Rows can be worked horizontally or diagonally.

* Left-handed people reverse "left" and "right."

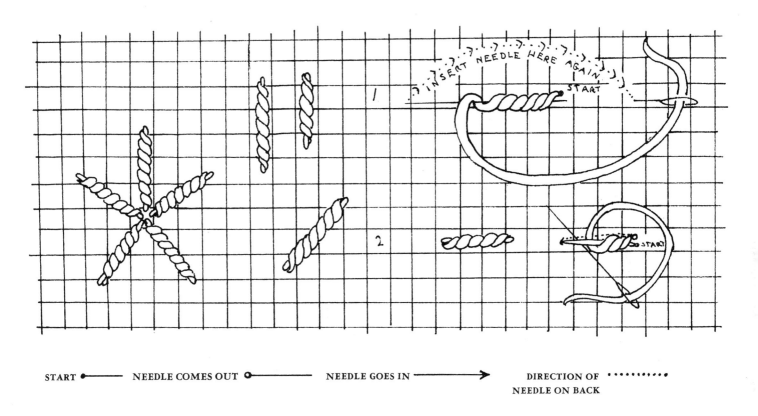

START ●——— NEEDLE COMES OUT ◦——— NEEDLE GOES IN ———▶ DIRECTION OF ••••••••••
NEEDLE ON BACK

BULLION KNOTS*

1. Bring yarn up from back where you wish left end of Bullion Knot to be, and insert needle where you wish right end of Bullion Knot to be. Bring tip of needle out part way in same hole as start of stitch. Don't pull needle and yarn through. Wrap yarn around needle tip, not too snug, as many times as will fill space to right of needle where it is under the canvas. Holding wrapped yarn carefully between thumb and finger of left hand, pull needle through, drawing yarn through part way. Still holding wrapped yarn carefully, turn over to the right and lay in place, drawing yarn the rest of the way through. Insert needle at right end of knot.

2. A simple way to produce the same thing is to make a stitch over site of Bullion Knot, bringing needle out at start of stitch. By passing the needle under this stitch several times, wrap yarn around stitch to cover it. Then insert needle into hole at end of stitch.

Limit length of Bullion Knot to ¾ inch. Knots do not need to follow lines of canvas threads. They are often worked on top of other stitching.

* Left-handed people reverse "left" and "right."

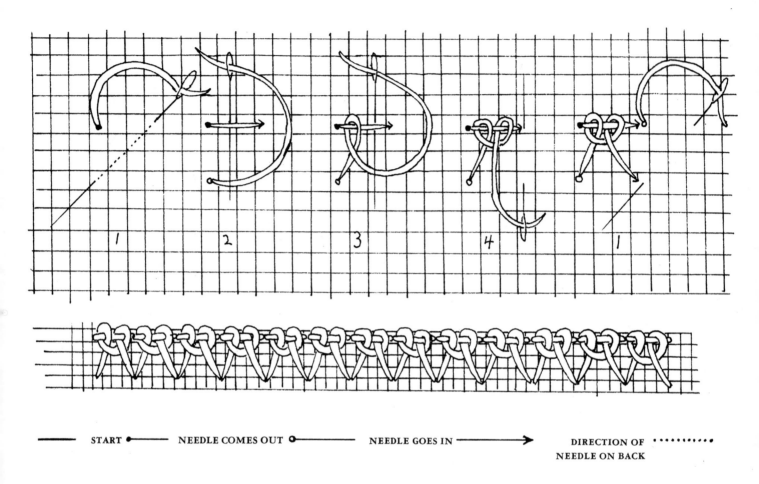

SORBELLO

Make a horizontal stitch over 3 (or 4) vertical threads (1), bringing needle out an equal number of threads below starting point. Holding yarn to right, pass the needle under horizontal stitch and over working strand (2). Repeat to right of step 2 (3). Insert needle 3 (or 4) threads below right end of first stitch (4) to form a square and bring it out at right end of first stitch. Repeat in horizontal rows from left to right. Heavy yarn is needed to cover canvas.

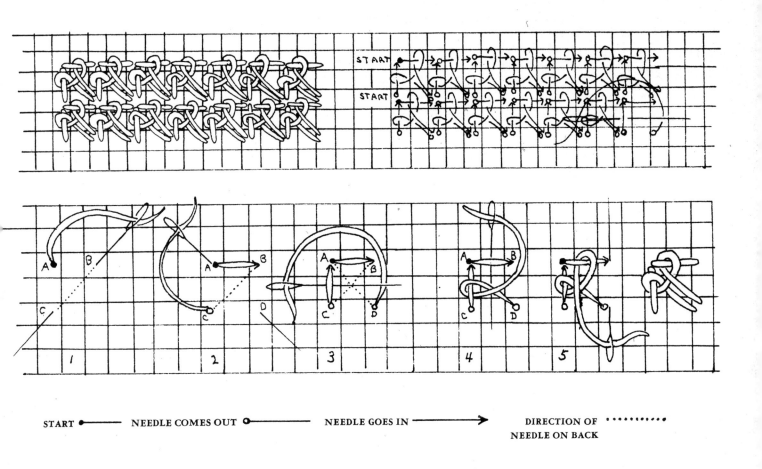

EASTERN, EGYPTIAN

Make a horizontal stitch over 2 threads (A–B), then a vertical stitch over 2 threads (C–A). Bring needle out at D, making a cross stitch on back of work. Holding working strand up, pass the needle under stitch C–A from left to right and over working strand. Do not penetrate the canvas. Now pass the needle under stitch A–B and over loop of third stitch. Insert needle at D and bring it out at A, ready for next stitch pattern. Leave steps 4 and 5 fairly loose. Start all rows at the left.

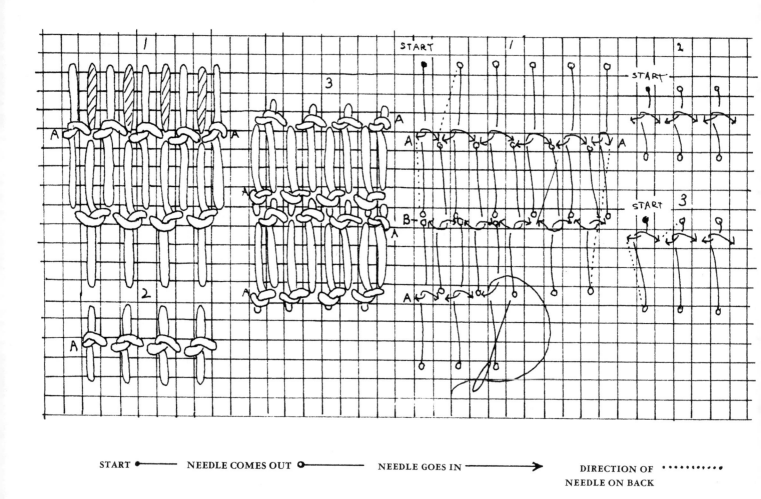

START ●———— NEEDLE COMES OUT ⦵———— NEEDLE GOES IN ————▶ DIRECTION OF •••••••••
NEEDLE ON BACK

INTERLACED

Vertical stitches are interwoven to form a braidlike line where they meet.

1. Starting at the top, make a stitch down over 4 threads, and 1 thread to the left. Bring the needle out 8 threads below start. Pass the needle under first stitch from right to left, and insert it 2 threads to the right of end of first stitch. Bring needle out 2 threads to the right of "start" and repeat.

   Second row. Start 8 threads down and 1 thread to the left of end of last stitch of row 1. Make first stitch up 4 threads and 1 thread to the right. Bring needle out in same hole as the ends of a pair of stitches of first row. Pass needle under first stitch, down right, and insert it 2 threads to the left of end of first stitch. The second row stitches fill spaces left between lower stitches of first row. Diagram 1 at left shows straight stitches used to fill spaces between top stitches of first row.

2. The shorter version is worked the same way except that the stitches cover 2 threads instead of 4.

3. In version 3 there is a short stitch over 1 intersection at the top, and a regular long stitch over 4 threads at the bottom.

   A. For compensating stitches for straight sides, omit the 1 thread to left and right at beginning and end of row. The first stitch covers just 4 threads down. In the last stitch of the row the needle is inserted 4 threads up from its beginning, after passing under top stitch.

   B. In diagram 1 the yarn must be taken through to the back and fastened, as the first stitch of the third row starts in the same hole as the end of last stitch of row 2.

154

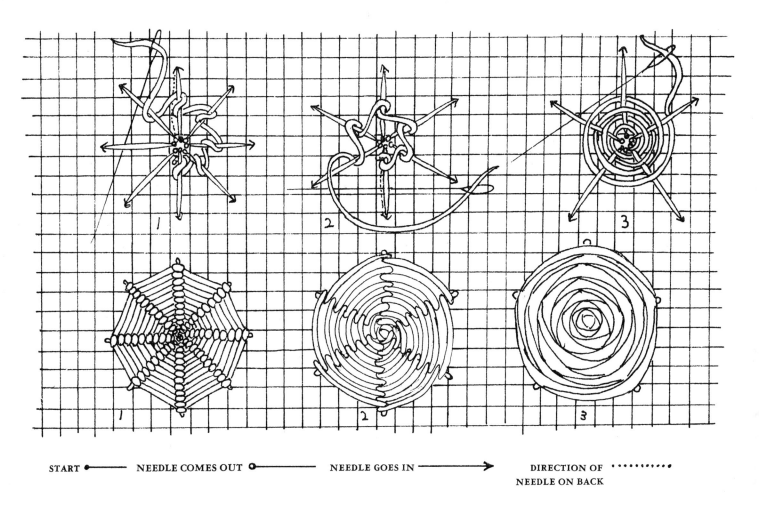

START ●———— NEEDLE COMES OUT ⊶———— NEEDLE GOES IN ————→ DIRECTION OF •••••••••
NEEDLE ON BACK

SPIDER WEBS 1, 2, & 3

1. Make a group of stitches like the spokes of a wheel, starting all stitches in the middle, any number, 5 to 8 works best. Bring needle out 1 hole below center. Pass needle under a spoke to the right. Then pass it under again, and also under the second spoke. Pass the needle under second spoke again and also under the third spoke. Continue around center, passing needle under each spoke twice. The spokes will be covered with raised ridges, with flat straight stitches between them.

2. Make spokes as in version 1. Bring needle out 1 hole below center. Carry yarn over first spoke and pass needle under it in a direction *opposite* to that of your spiral. Carry yarn over first spoke and then over second spoke. Pass needle under second spoke. Continue around center until spokes are covered. This version of Spider Web is the "back side" of version 1.

3. Make spokes as in versions 1 and 2. This time you must have an *uneven* number. Bring needle out 1 hole below center. Pass needle over first stitch, under the second, over the third, etc. Continue to weave yarn over and under spokes around center. If the spokes are somewhat unevenly placed it won't show on finished web. In spite of the length of the outside stitches, they stay in place. If fairly heavy yarn is used the spiral of yarn passing over and under the spokes covers the spokes completely and produces a pleasing round shape, raised near the edges and slightly depressed in the center.

The finished products of these 3 versions of Spider Web are far more attractive than the pen-and-ink drawings.

BIBLIOGRAPHY

Canvas Work and Design, by Jennifer Gray. London: B. T. Batsford, Ltd., 1960.

Canvas Embroidery, by Hebe Cox. London: Mills and Boon Limited, 1960.

Canvas Work, by M. A. Gibbon. London: G. Bell and Sons, Ltd., 1965.

Creative Canvas Embroidery, by Bucky King. New York: Hearthside Press, 1963.

Encyclopedia of Needlework, by Thérèse de Dillmont. Mullhouse, France.

Ideas for Canvas Work, by Mary Rhodes. Newton, Massachusetts: Charles T. Batsford, 1970.

Needlepoint for Beginners. New York: McCall Corporation, 1967.

Needlework Stitches, by Barbara Snook. New York: Crown Publishers, Inc., 1963.

New Methods in Needlepoint, by Hope Hanley. New York: Charles Schribner' Sons, 1968.

"New Stitches for Canvas Embroidery," by John Gleave in *Embroidery,* summer 1971, published quarterly by The Embroiders' Guild, 73 Wimpole Street, London, England.

Samplers and Stitches, by Mrs. Archibald Christis London: B. T. Batsford, Ltd., first edition, 1920; seventh edition, 1959.

INDEX